My Paranorm

One Man's Obsession

By Rick Waid

My Paranormal Journey: One Man's Obsession
By Rick Waid
Cover design by Michelle Schultz

ISBN-13: 978-1508706939
ISBN-10: 150870693X

10 9 8 7 6 5 4 3 2 1

"There are reasons for exploring into new territories and breaking through current boundaries."

–Rick Waid

Contents

Introduction

My name is Rick Waid, and I am a paranormal investigator. I have had an obsession with the paranormal for many years. It started after I watched a ghost-hunting show on TV. Then my obsession with the paranormal exploded after I had my first personal experience with what I believed to be a spirit communicating directly with me.

During my paranormal journey, I also discovered I had hidden psychic abilities that blossomed as I investigated the strange and unusual sites around my hometown. But that is another story. In these pages, I share with you how my paranormal journey began and where it led me: to an obsession with the unknown. An obsession that cost me friends. An obsession that almost destroyed my family and my job. An obsession that brought me an understanding that there is more to our world than we can explain.

Rick Waid

During my journey, I have investigated with groups, friends, and family members. I have investigated alone. I have also broken some rules along the way. To anyone reading this book, please take caution.

I am not advocating that anyone investigate alone. I am not advocating that anyone trespass onto private property, abandoned or otherwise.

It can be extremely dangerous to investigate alone. I have no excuse for putting myself in danger, other than I did it because that is where my obsession took me. I let my fascination with the unknown lead me to lie to my family, and it almost cost me my job.

I ask that each of you investigate safely and in the company of others who can back you up. Always get permission before entering a location, and always research the potential dangers of each location that you intend to investigate. Have a plan in place for each possible danger that you could encounter on location. And, finally, always respect the property, as well as the spirits, during your search for the paranormal.

My journey unfolded as I think it was meant to. Did I make mistakes? Yes, many of them. But I hope that I can share my lessons learned to help others who are on their own paranormal journey.

–Rick Waid

Chapter 1:
My First Experience — Capturing Paranormal Activity on Video

My obsession with the paranormal began in fall 2005 when my wife thought it would be a good idea to record a ghost-hunting show. She thought it would be cool for us to watch it together. What she didn't realize at the time was how this one fateful idea would lead to so much pain and suffering, especially for her personally!

I was somewhat spellbound by the ghost-hunting show. I admit it was neat to see people trying to catch ghosts on camera, as well as watching them run when some strange noise was heard or a flash of light occurred. Sometimes it was more funny than scary.

We watched the show for at least one season, and we never missed any episodes because we recorded them all. It fascinated me when the team on TV encountered strange events that they couldn't explain. It was all so exciting! And it was almost excruciating to have to wait an entire week before the next show aired. But it was worth the wait.

Then one day my son, Andrew, came over to tell me about an old house that he knew of at the end of a local street. He said it looked really creepy. So, we decided to check it out later that night at about 10 p.m.

My son and son-in-law, Rick, as well as a few others, gathered that night. We headed out and worked our way down the road to see the old house. It was different than any other old house. There was something special about it. The house was a two-story white home from the early 1900s, standing ominously at the end of the road. It looked completely abandoned, and it seemed like no one had lived there in a long time. The doors were locked and the windows covered with shutters. There was an old, tattered couch in the front yard, and the surrounding area looked extremely creepy, even scary.

The backyard was all woods and very swampy. Just standing there gave me chills. As we walked around the house, everyone was goofing off and having fun. On a whim, I looked up and saw a second-floor shutter open. I asked if there were any spirits present that would like to communicate, and if so, to please close the shutter.

As soon as I said it, the shutter promptly closed. It freaked me out, but at the same time, I was in awe at what had just happened. I decided to immediately go back home and grab my video camera, hoping the spirit would still be there when I returned.

As I drove back to the old house after retrieving my camera, I was already filming in night vision. I continued to film the front of the house as we drove slowly onto the gravel driveway. Creepy feelings abounded. My son-in-law and I got out of my car, and I asked whatever spirits were present to open the shutter, which had previously closed on its own.

The shutter proceeded to open slowly. We could hear the creaking sound as the shutter opened on its own. As it opened, we exchanged the following dialogue:

"Oh, no way!" my son-in-law, Rick, said.

"That is exactly what I am saying, dude," I whispered.

"Oh, no way," Rick said again.

"There is something here," I whispered.

"There is no wind," Rick said.

"There is no wind," I confirmed. I couldn't believe what I was seeing.

"You better be recording this!"

"I am."

There was no doubt in our minds that this was a ghost or spirit communicating with us. Once I arrived back home, I showed my daughter, Chorissa, and my wife, Anne, the footage. They both claimed the wind caused the shutter to open and close, but I knew the wind was not to blame.

The abandoned house where the shutter on the second-story window opened and closed on command. (Screen capture from video.)

This one shutter closing and later opening on its own impacted me deeply, so much so that I immediately started on a journey to prove that there are always ghosts and spirits around the living. My mission was to prove that if you are willing to give these spirits the attention they sometimes seek, they will usually communicate back.

I still watched the ghost-hunting show during the infancy of my obsession with the paranormal. I gathered up all the tips I could on what I needed to try and experiment with on my ghost-hunting trips.

It was around Halloween that this life-change was happening to me. I heard on a radio station in my surrounding area that they were asking for paranormal information or stories that people had encountered. I called into the station and talked to Dave Justus, explaining to him a bit about my video capturing the shutter activity. He wanted to see the video and asked me to come down in the morning to show off my so-called proof of the paranormal. I was very excited about going on the radio show.

I knew Dave from another radio show in town where I participated in a fear factor contest for Creed concert tickets. I won by eating and chewing three night crawlers the fastest. I smoked all of the competitors and won tickets to eat with the band and meet them backstage.

I went downtown to the studios the next morning, and Dave and his co-host put me on air with them. I showed my video to them. You should have seen their faces after they saw the shutter door open; it really gave them goose bumps. They thought if there was any real proof of the existence of ghosts, then this was as close as it gets. They agreed to have one of their interns come with me back to the abandoned house to see if we could recreate the occurrence again.

I actually knew the intern, because I had shown up at the station previously to try and win prizes for completing various stunts. As soon as we got back to the abandoned house, I began rewinding my video camera so I wouldn't record over my previous recordings of the shutter opening. At that moment, the shutter opened before both of our eyes. We couldn't record it because the video camera was rewinding. Unfortunately, I missed capturing another great moment on my camera. The intern called into the station and explained what just took place. I asked the spirits to open the shutter again, but nothing happened.

I made plans with Dave, the radio show host, to go out that night and research the local graveyard. Rick and I met up with Dave at the exit ramp by the graveyard. We drove down the road about a mile and turned into the dark, creepy graveyard. We all walked around and tried to see if anything would make its presence known. At one point, we gathered and held an impromptu séance. With nothing happening, we decided to leave for the night. It seemed that our investigation at the cemetery was a bust.

Rick and I decided to go back to the abandoned house again one Friday night. But when we arrived, our camera broke. It would not turn on. But that didn't stop that shutter door from doing what it had to do. We gave different commands, and the shutter followed every one of them, from going very slow to very fast. We asked it to stop in the middle of its movement, and it did! Unfortunately, there was no recording to prove it since the camera wasn't working.

What an exciting experience we had that night! Rick and I wondered who the spirit was that we were communicating with. Later that night, we had a heavy windstorm. When I checked on the house the next morning, the wind had blown the shutter door off. To have such amazing activity at the home, and then to have this happen was very disappointing.

As I looked more at the video footage, I noticed that a light had turned on in the home while we were videotaping. However, we verified that there was no electricity available at the location. Even though the shutter was not there anymore, I still wondered if I could capture some energy with my digital camera. I ended up going back to that old house many more times, taking pictures and hoping something would show up. I did get strange orb-looking objects on film that I thought were ghosts or spirits floating through the night air. Every time I took a picture, they were there. I saw on the ghost show that these objects could sometimes be considered spirit orbs. Other times they could be dust or bugs. It seemed to me that the location might contain a portal that spirits could utilize to come and go.

I took the pictures home, and my wife said there was nothing paranormal in them. It was almost as if she knew trouble was coming her way. From the start, my wife never believed that the events I was capturing were paranormal. She said there were explanations for everything. I have to admit that she was usually right, but I was hoping not this time.

I didn't have any answers about what I was experiencing, but I still very much wanted to go back out to find more proof. I did some research on the old house and found out that the Native Americans in the area would bring their canoes up to the house. Also, I uncovered that an old saloon used to sit next to the house. I asked around town, and not many people knew about anything strange happening there. But I did hear from a librarian that there was a young girl who stayed in the room with the shutter on the window. The young girl was said to never come out of the house.

At one time, the town's fire department used the old salon for drills. And one day they burned it down. Now there is an expressway off ramp at that location.

Chapter 2:
A Graveyard Investigation

My paranormal obsession was in full swing now. I decided to make my next journey one to an old Native American graveyard that I had heard about. I anxiously prepared for my lone investigation, getting my digital camera ready and hoping to capture something unknown and unexplainable.

When I arrived at the cemetery, I was already scared. It was a graveyard, and growing up graveyards weren't a place you wanted to venture into at night. I slowly walked into the cemetery in the dark night. It was quiet, but I could hear noises coming from the back of the graveyard, adding to my apprehension. It didn't take long before I actually ran back to my car, filled with fear. I swiftly got in my car and drove home.

Going alone into a place like that was very frightening for me. I have to admit; I get very scared watching scary movies or when people jump out of places and try to scare me.

I soon got my video camera back from the repair shop. I decided that I was going back to that graveyard and conquering my fear. I was excited and eager to go back. So, one night, on a whim, I headed out. I arrived at the cemetery with my headlights off and drove through the entire area taking pictures and videotaping. I finally got out of my car and left the video camera on a tombstone, hoping something would cross its path.

That night I stayed in the graveyard for about an hour. Then I decided I wanted to look over my evidence. When I got home I loaded all of my pictures onto my computer. Most of them were very dark, so I decided to lighten them up. When I did, I noticed a few orbs in my shots. Not small ones, but huge orbs that sometimes took up the entire frame of the photo. As I carefully looked over my photos in more detail, I noticed what looked like an old lady standing behind a tree. In the same picture I spotted a boy's face. Wow, was this a good discovery!

While investigating a cemetery, I captured what looked
like a spirit standing to the right of this tree.

Another Friday had come, and I got everything ready to go back to the graveyard. When I arrived that night, I parked my car and got out. To my dismay, none of my equipment seemed to work. It was like something was shutting things down, and my camera wouldn't turn on. Feeling like I was not alone, I got back into my car, but it wouldn't start. I began to feel scared once again. I considered calling my wife to come pick me up, but she would have been really mad.

I calmed myself down, and after about five minutes everything started working again. However, I was not feeling comfortable at all that night, so I left.

Later that night, I read on the Internet that investigators usually capture paranormal activity just before dawn. I didn't know how true this information was, but I decided to give it a shot.

The first cemetery I investigated alone. During a return visit, my equipment and car failed.

Saturday arrived, and I went out a little before dawn and started taking pictures and videotaping at the graveyard. This time I asked the spirit to show itself as I held my video camera still. Later, as I looked back at the footage, when I asked the question I could see an energy ball appear on the camera. It was moving so fast that it left in its path eight or nine lighter energy balls. I had never seen anything like that before! It was very hard to see, and I had to watch it a few times, but it was there.

I soon brought a few friends to the graveyard, hoping they would experience the paranormal. Most of my friends just laughed at what I was doing and never believed any of it. I believe that they never really cared enough about having an experience, and I think the spirits knew this. That is why they never materialized for my friends.

One day, I brought my son with me to the cemetery. We hung out for about an hour and a half, hoping to get a cool picture or capture something on videotape. Unfortunately, we never saw anything in the graveyard or in any of the pictures.

Investigating the cemetery with my son
(holding the video camera).

At this point, I really wanted to research another home, so I decided to head back to the "shutter door home" for more research.

Chapter 3:
The Woman in the Mirror & The Old Hotel

One evening, my daughter, Chorissa, called to tell me that her husband, Rick, had seen "a woman" in their mirror at home. It scared them both so much that they decided to stay at my house. Chorissa told me that she previously had a dream, and the female in the dream was the same woman that Rick saw in the mirror.

I packed up my equipment to go over and research their place. When I got there, everything was quiet and I began to ask questions, such as, "Are you here?" "Why are you here?" and, "What do you want?" I didn't seem to be getting any response, but as I was leaving, there were three doors open to the bathroom and two bedrooms. As I walked toward the entry door, all three of those doors shut at the same time. This was obviously paranormal activity of some sort, and I instantly knew that I wanted to investigate and research the home more thoroughly.

The house where my son-in-law saw a spirit in the mirror.

I asked around and found out that a woman was found dead in her bed inside the house. She had been there for about a week before someone found her. They ruled the death a suicide, but some people said there was more to the story.

I came back a few more times and brought some neighbors over as well. During one investigation of the home, I took a picture and noticed that there was something black in the picture that I couldn't account for. I asked the neighbors and my daughter if they could identify the object, but none of us could figure out what it was.

I went back a few days later, and I figured out what the black object was. It was my finger. Lesson learned!

Chorissa stayed there for about a year, and nothing else unusual happened after that. Since she was not a believer in the paranormal, maybe something was telling her that what Rick saw in the mirror, as well as her dream, was real and not just a bunch of nonsense.

Just after investigating Chorissa and Rick's house, I took on another paranormal adventure. Across the street and a little way down the road from my house was another old, abandoned home. I thought I would give this one a try.

Around 11:30 p.m. one night, I packed up my equipment and headed out. It was great that my wife didn't say much about me going out late at night, and I thanked her very much for that. I was excited for another great night investigating, and when I got to the old house, there was no one else on the street. It seemed everyone was asleep. I decided to take pictures and see what I could capture.

Everything was going great until the owner of the house, who apparently lived across the street, came out and approached me.

"What are you doing?" he asked.

"I'm ghost hunting," I said.

"Kids come around here all the time and have destroyed the property," he explained, adding that the structure was his family's house and there had never been any ghosts there.

"Check out the old hotel on the next street. It should be open, because they are remodeling it," he said.

I thanked him and never went back again. But I did take his advice and went to the hotel the next night. When I went ghost hunting, I would scope each place out during the day to see how much activity was happening inside and outside of the location. What I was doing was wrong, because I did not have permission to go onto the premises. But this did not stop me. My obsession was completely out of control.

An old hotel that was being remodeled. An orb can be seen in the middle of the picture.

As I watched the workers who were helping to remodel the hotel, they finally left at around five p.m., with no one coming back again until the next morning. It was a Wednesday night when I returned to the hotel. As I arrived at the location, I was scared out of my wits. I hadn't worked up enough courage to face a ghost yet.

They were converting the hotel into an apartment complex. The door was open, and I went in. I immediately smelled that musky smell that houses often get when no one has lived there in a while. I checked out the upstairs first, taking random pictures and videotaping. As I was getting ready to go downstairs, I saw a cop come down the street! I turned off the camera light and stood still, hoping he didn't see me. I am glad I didn't park on the road by the hotel. Instead, I parked a little ways away by the dumpster across the tracks.

As I watched the policeman make his rounds, I got spooked and left the property. I decided not to come back.

I think now is a good time to reiterate what I said in my introduction to this book. I made some mistakes when I was completely obsessed with paranormal investigation. Not obtaining permission to investigate certain locations was one of these mistakes. In hindsight, this was not a smart move, and I caution others to never trespass onto a location. I learned from my mistakes, and I hope that these lessons learned will help others.

Chapter 4:
My First Audio Recorder

It was now getting close to Christmas, and it had become a tradition to travel north to celebrate. Even though we were away from home for the holidays, I couldn't wait until nighttime so I could start researching the area. Christmas morning arrived, and we all opened up our presents. I received a very special gift that I will never forget.

It was an audio recorder, a gift from my wife. She loved me so much that she got me the best gift I would ever receive. It was the start of a new journey, one that I was ready to take. I read on the Internet that if you really want to hear ghost voices, you must conduct EVP sessions for at least 10 minutes every day to become accustomed to hearing the EVPs. The information I came across suggested that I sit down, ask questions, and after about a month I would have trained my ears to hear what others couldn't. This was another "toy" I could bring out with me to connect in a different way with the spirits.

Recording audio during an investigation.

This one small gift, the audio recorder, sent my paranormal obsession into high gear. I was headed on a journey that would change my life forever — for good and bad.

My immediate goal was to take my audio recorder back to the old hotel. Once we arrived home from our holiday trip, that very night I was out on the prowl, ready to hear the ghosts speak.

When I got back to the hotel, I left my recorder on the steps, hoping I would hear something, maybe even phantom footsteps. I went outside by a big tree and sat there, praying that I would be able to hear or see ghosts. I was so excited that I waited only 15 minutes and then gathered my cameras and recorder. I headed back to my car and listened to the audio recorder to see if I could hear anything I might have captured. Five minutes into listening to the audio, I heard a weird scream. It was wild!

I had to listen to it over and over to make sure it was still there. I couldn't believe my ears! I knew something must have happened, but how could this be? I didn't hear a scream when I was sitting outside.

Once I got the video footage home, I reviewed it thoroughly. I noticed what looked like orbs on the videotape, but nothing else. It was a little disappointing after the scream I had captured, but at least I still had that!

I returned to the old hotel the next night, but before I could even get started investigating, I spotted a policeman circling the neighborhood. Disappointed, I left the location and headed home.

Chapter 5:
The Pet Store & The Old Mill

One Friday night I drove down to the pet store, which wasn't very far from where the old hotel was. I decided to leave my audio recorder at the base of an old sign at the Old Mill that stood near the pet store. The mill was over 150 years old. For some reason, I felt confident that no one would steal my recorder.

Not really thinking that I would catch anything paranormal on the recorder, I went into the grocery store down the road for a bit before returning to the pet store. I picked up my recorder and began driving home. As I drove, I started listening to the audio, and what I heard sent shivers through my body.

I could hear a man say, "Let me be. Leave me alone."

Thoughts immediately started swirling through my head. Was I doing something wrong or bad? What was the spirit really saying? Was the spirit communicating with me personally, or did I record a voice from the past, one that keeps looping time after time? I thought it was very strange that the voice was captured during the brief time that I had left the recorder on. This was all new to me. What was I really hearing?

That Saturday morning, I let my wife hear the audio I had captured. She thought it was some kind of cell phone conversation or police radio interference. She didn't believe it was a ghost imprint.

But it seemed that the more I researched the paranormal, the more spirits, or something, seemed to gravitate toward me. It almost seemed like they wanted to talk to me. This all was a new part of the path I was on, and I was obsessed with it all. I thought about the paranormal 24/7 and couldn't get it out of my head.

I visited the pet store again, and this time I left the recorder overnight, picking it up the next morning very early before the sun rose. In my job, I drive a far distance for work, so I always had time to listen to my recordings when I was on the road. This particular time I heard people walking, not a few footsteps, but a lot of steps. It went on for almost an hour. However, there was no one walking around at the pet shop. It was closed long before I left the recorder. Also, there was nothing else open around the location, so there would be no reason for anyone to be walking around the area at night.

I couldn't make sense of all the footsteps recorded! Could I have captured the past replaying itself from when the mill was in operation? What I captured on the recorder seemed impossible, but it was there. I knew there was a message in what I had captured, but I couldn't explain it … yet.

The next night I decided to pour flour on the ground surrounding the signpost to see if anyone disturbed it. Later, when I retrieved my recorder, I noticed that the flour was undisturbed. There were no footprints to be found. So, to my surprise, when I reviewed my audio I again heard the footsteps.

I soon found out that the area was home to strange activity. The next time I visited the pet store, it was during the day. As I walked into the store, I immediately overheard a conversation taking place by the store employees. The topic being discussed was paranormal activity. Weird occurrences were happening in the store at all hours.

Things would be moved from one location to another, among other unexplainable events.

The site of the Old Mill and pet store where I captured audio phenomena.

As I joined the conversation, the employees told me the pet shop was haunted. I excitedly filled them in on my recent investigations and revealed that I had been recording disembodied footsteps outside the shop. I even let them listen to my recordings. I asked them if I could bring my equipment to the store and leave it there overnight. They agreed, but I had to be there early the next morning to pick up my recorder before the owner came in. I came back that night and set up my equipment and recorder where I felt there would be little noise from the animals.

The next morning I arrived to pick up my equipment, excited to see if I caught anything. I told the employees that I would get back to them as soon as possible. When I reviewed the evidence, at times the animals would become very quiet, as if something was happening in the store. And when the dogs started to bark, there were no other sounds. I didn't get much evidence that night, but I did hear what sounded like some of the cages opening and closing while no one was in the store.

About a week later, my wife and I were coming home from a date when we stopped by the Old Mill sign again. I asked if there were any spirits that would like to talk on the recorder, and just as I finished speaking, a streetlight burned out. Even though I recorded at that site many times after that, I never captured any more activity by the sign. It was almost as if the spirits left when the light burned out.

Can spirits affect objects when trying to communicate, as they seemed to do by turning off this light by the Old Mill after I asked them a question?

This setback did not affect my passion for the paranormal. By this point in my journey, I had already captured a lot of strange and unexplainable activity on audio and in my photos and video. I felt compelled to get what was happening to me out to more people. So I looked on the Internet for some kind of group or someone to talk to about what was happening to me. I immediately found a site called Haunted Voices, which hosted a Web radio show. People could call into the show and chat online about their personal experiences and what was happening to them. I called in and spoke to the show's host, Todd Bates, about my investigations, the EVPs I was capturing, and my mission to find out more about the paranormal.

"If you are getting that many voices, the spirits are most likely attracted to you for some reason," Todd said.

After thinking about Todd's words for a bit, I realized I might know why the spirits spoke openly to me so often. Many people warned me not to investigate by myself. They said I could fall and get hurt or that a spirit could take over my body. I've also heard many ghost hunters say that there should always be two people investigating together at all times for safety reasons and also so that each can document any activity that occurs and compare their notes. One person's information is not as credible as multiple accounts of the same activity. But was it possible that the spirits were not intimidated by me as a lone investigator? Did they feel more open and less threatened to come forward?

Todd at Haunted Voices gave me some new ideas on how to reach spirits and get more proof of the paranormal that I so desperately wanted.

Chapter 6:
The Old School House

During my day job, I sometimes travel hundreds of miles away from home. This was also true in the early years of my paranormal obsession. And during these drives, I was always on the lookout for any unusual or creepy locations to investigate, including abandoned sites. On one drive, I spotted on old school house that was abandoned. I knew instantly that I would investigate the site. It called to me.

It wasn't long before I found myself in front of the abandoned property. As I approached the building, I noticed that it was boarded up pretty good, but I found the back door open. I was eager to start investigating. Would I be able to hear phantom children talking and playing around the school? I hoped so.

The old school house.

I decided to employ an investigative technique recommended by Todd from Haunted Voices. I turned the handle on the door, played with the outside latch, stomped my feet, and knocked on the door. I then turned on the recorder, set it down inside the back door, and returned a couple of hours later. I took the recorder and returned home to find out if I captured any unexplainable voices or other activity. Sure enough, at one point in the recording, I could faintly hear the handle turning on the door, the latch moving, feet stomping, and knocking on the door, in that order.

This threw me for a loop! Was I really hearing this? Did a spirit respond to my initial contact by imitating it in return? Or was my mind playing tricks and I was simply hearing what I wanted to hear?

At the old school house.

I returned to the school house the next night to try and contact any spirits present and find out what information they could give me. As I investigated the basement, I asked for the spirits to make a sound. As soon as I asked, I heard something in the ductwork. It could have been an animal, but it seemed to respond to me as soon as I asked. From my past experiences, this — to me — was a sign.

I decided to leave my recorder overnight on a ledge in the school house where no one would see it. I would pick it up on my way to work the next day. But when I arrived the next morning, the recorder was on but not recording. The batteries had a little bit of charge left, so I changed the batteries and began to listen. It had recorded for one hour and that was all. But what I heard startled me. It sounded like someone was playing with the recorder, kind of like they had never seen anything like it before and were curious about it. Then the recorder stopped recording.

That night I called into the Haunted Voices show and told Todd about the things that were happening and how it seemed like someone or something turned off my recorder. Todd told me that he believed I had a "crack" in my aura and that when the spirits and ghosts see that light they basically come running to me.

I continued to call into Haunted Voices to talk with Todd and his guests. I would often play on his show the spirit voices that I had captured on my recorder. I also listened to other guests who had recorded EVPs. At the time, I didn't have many people to turn to who believed that I was in contact with something supernatural. Todd was the only person who would listen and actually help me deal with what was going on. It was like he actually knew the spirits would respond to what I was asking them to do. I owe so much to Todd. Some people believe they are not gifted, but Todd's advice was a gift in its own way. He is a very calm person and a great listener. I was a constant presence around the show for a while, listening and learning as much as I could.

Then I moved on to another part of my journey. I believe everybody has a story — their own journey. And at this point, my journey evolved. But, it seemed that I was allowing my paranormal obsession to drag me into even more dangerous circumstances.

One night, we had a big storm with a lot of snow. Later the same day, I drove by the school house on my way to my last job for the day. I decided that I would set my recorder back into the school house. So I waded through three feet of snow to put the recorder inside the window, where it wouldn't get any snow on it.

As I got back into my Durango after leaving the recorder, I went too far to the right and immediately went into a deep decline. My vehicle stopped short of almost tipping over. I was leaning dangerously far to the right. So, I placed a call to my towing company, and while I was on the phone a truck stopped by to help me. We hooked a chain onto my Durango but couldn't budge it. So I thanked the kind man for his time and told him I was on the phone with a towing company.

Five minutes later another truck came by and asked to help. I told him about the other truck stopping to help and that we had no luck. He still thought he could get me out. So we tried the process again, and he asked me not to give it any gas and he would pull me out. I was out within a few seconds. I could not believe it. As I took his chains back to him, he handed me a brochure about getting right with the Lord.

"You need to stop what you are doing," he told me.

Those words still ring in my ears today.

His message put a bit of fear in me! What was I doing? There was no way he could have known what I was doing. Or is it possible that he did know?

I went back and retrieved my recorder and never went back to that old school house again.

Near where my car almost tipped over by the old school.

My wife was very upset with me, because it took me a long time to do my last job that day. And when I called her to tell her I was stuck in the snow, she asked me if I was ghost hunting. I told her I was not, and this lie was the first of what would become many lies. I developed a bad habit of lying to my wife about my ghost-hunting escapades. I was obsessed, and nothing or no one would stop me.

That night after I made it home from my time stuck in the snow, I began thinking again about what the stranger had said to me. It made me wonder about so many things. Was I doing the right thing by investigating the paranormal? I thought that maybe I should start asking the spirits specific questions, like whether they were a good or bad spirit. I decided to take a short break from investigating to regroup and better prepare for my next adventure. I needed to strategize.

But something else started happening to me soon after I received my warning from the stranger. When I would fill up my gas tank, there would be a bible on the pump. When I would use the bathroom at gas stations, there would be a bible in the bathroom. Was someone trying to send me a message, perhaps even God?

Chapter 7:
I Joined a Paranormal Team

At this point in my journey, I decided to join a paranormal team. I found a team that seemed professional and friendly. A requirement of joining this particular team was showing up at the team meetings and the scheduled investigations. I officially joined the group as a medium and an audio specialist. How I would fit in, I didn't know yet, but I was going to try.

During my first meeting, we talked about how to approach an investigation and what steps each team member would take. After investigating alone for so long, it was nice to share information and ideas with others. My first investigation with the group was at a team member's home. We all met on a Friday night at a pre-designated meeting place and then drove together to the location in one vehicle.

When we arrived at the house, it was cold and very windy. We all went into the home, organized our equipment, and began the hunt. Our process was that we all would take a seat on the enclosed porch, and one person at a time would go through the house and see what they could find — one team member with a video camera, one with a recorder, and one using their mediumistic abilities. The same rotation went on until all the "sensitive" investigators had their own story.

When it was my turn to investigate, all of the equipment began to act up. Static seriously affected the walkie talkies. The most sensitive investigators on the case said there was "something" going on with me. I went through every area asking questions with my recorder. Then we all sat down at the table and compared notes. What we were trying to accomplish with this method was to find the paranormal hotspots at the location. We then divided into two groups, with one group going to one identified hotspot and the other group going to the second hotspot. We then rotated locations.

Before dividing into groups to investigate, we sat down to compare notes.

At the end of the investigation, we all came together in the same room and the sensitives and psychics told their story of what had happened. I recorded the session. I have to admit … I didn't know the team very well, and I had a hard time believing in each psychic's "gift." I had never investigated like this before, and what they were saying was a bit hard to believe — until later when I played the audio back. Sarah, one of the psychics, was right every time she said a name. The information was verified by the voices captured on the recorder. She also said that a male spirit was cussing and trying to come on to her. I had to keep myself from laughing when she said it, but then I again verified everything she said after listening to the evidence we captured. I finally believed that she really did have a gift.

That night we captured more than 30 spirit voices, and all of our mediums' stories were confirmed.

The next day I gathered all the audio recordings together and sent them out to the team. I was surprised when they didn't seem very interested in the audio, even though it backed up everything our team's psychics had revealed during the investigation. I asked the team leader to put the audio on their Website, but he never did.

While I did not understand why they didn't post their evidence for others to hear and see, I was still impressed with some of the members' psychic abilities. Unfortunately, the team began to argue about who was the most talented, and I didn't like being around people who couldn't be a true team. I tried to talk to the owner about what was going on, but it seemed like half of the team was solid while the other half was dismissive.

I ultimately decided that the group was not for me, and I left the team shortly thereafter. It was at this time that I began investigating on my own again.

Chapter 8:
Why I Didn't Meet Sylvia Browne

My paranormal obsession took its toll. I spent less time with my family and friends and more time alone investigating in my spare time. My wife was still there for me, even though she was having a hard time dealing with what I was doing. But I had to find someone who would really listen to what was happening during my investigations; I knew this would be hard to do.

One day I was watching *The Montel Williams Show*, which featured psychic Sylvia Browne, who helped individuals with the types of questions I had. I decided to email the show and was surprised when they actually called me back for more information. I sent them more details of what I had encountered along with as much proof as I could find of my personal experiences.

Again to my surprise, the show arranged for me to meet Sylvia. It was in the middle of December when they gave me the meeting date. I told my entire family the news, and everyone was excited. When it got closer to the meeting, the show's producers called and wanted to change my story to fit the show. I was not happy with how they were creating a story that might not be true. They wanted to infer that my mother was trying to communicate with me from the afterlife, which I had no direct proof of. I thought about it for a while, and in the end I agreed with them because I desperately wanted to find answers to what I was experiencing.

The week before my plane ride, the producers had an issue with the show and canceled everything. I knew that maybe I was not seeing what was really happening. Maybe these spirits didn't want me to show anybody what I had really seen and heard. Today, I still believe this is what was happening at the time.

MOUNTAIN MOVERS PRODUCTIONS, INC.
433 W. 53rd Street
New York, NY 10019

AGREEMENT TO APPEAR

The following is my agreement to appear on "The Montel Williams Show" (the "Series") on the date and time indicated below, or at another date and time to be determined by the producers, subject to my availability:

APPEARANCE DATE: APPEARANCE TIME:

1. I represent to you that I have not previously appeared on a television talk show. I further represent and warrant that I will not be interviewed by or appear on **ANY OTHER TELEVISION TALK OR VARIETY SHOW** including and without limitation OPRAH WINFREY, MAURY POVICH, JERRY SPRINGER, ELLEN, LIVE WITH REGIS AND KELLY, THE VIEW, MARTHA STEWART, THE TYRA BANKS SHOW, DR.PHIL, THE DR. KEITH ABLOW SHOW, THE GREG BEHRENDT SHOW, RACHEL RAY, and THE MEGAN MULALLY SHOW until such time as the episode of the Show on which I appear is initially broadcast, or ninety days from the date of my appearance, whichever first occurs.

2. I understand that: (a) I will be advised of travel information and arrangements and additional details regarding the episode taping schedule by telephone; (b) my appearance is subject to cancellation or postponement by the producers at any time for any reason without recourse; and (c) I will be required to sign your Program Appearance Release and such other releases (the "Releases") as you may request before the taping of the Series, and I warrant that I will sign the Releases as needed.

3. I agree to pay, and to indemnify and hold harmless Mountain Movers Productions, Inc. ("MMP"), the producer of the Series, from and against any and all costs, expenses and liabilities which MMP may incur, including, but not limited to, all production and travel costs incurred by MMP, for the breach of any representations and warranties as contained herein and/or if I fail or refuse to appear on the Series without good cause.

4. I hereby indemnify you, your officers, directors, agents, affiliated stations, distributors and licensees against any claims against you arising out of my appearance on the Series and/or my acts or statements made off-air and/or on the Series. I hereby release you from any loss, claims or injuries that may occur arising out of my participation in and/or appearance on the Series and/or its permitted uses.

5. I acknowledge and agree that this agreement shall be deemed made and performed in New York, New York, whose substantive laws shall govern and whose courts shall have exclusive jurisdiction over any dispute relating to this agreement.

SIGNED:_____ DATE:

PRINT NAME:

PHONE:

ADDRESS:

OTHER PHONE:_____ SS#:

If guest is under eighteen years of age: I approve the terms of this release and guarantee performance by my child or ward.

(Signature of Parent or Legal Guardian)

The Agreement to Appear form that The Montel Williams Show sent to me.

Chapter 9:
The Spirit House

My sister-in-law, Shell, called me one day and said she had found a cool-looking old house while out on a bike ride. It was just off the bike route. She said she had actually ventured inside and come across some really old things, nothing of value, but it made her feel uneasy. So, of course, I had to check it out, and I was again on the road to another investigation.

As I was driving into the area, I immediately got goose bumps on the left side of my head. I knew I was close. I crossed over where the old railroad tracks were, and then I saw it, hidden by trees. There were no houses by it, so I parked in the old driveway by the barn and looked around to see if someone was outside. There was no one around. As I walked through the tall grass, I hoped there were no hidden wells that I could fall into. If I did, I would never be seen again.

An abandoned house where I captured spirit activity.

I went around back, hoping no one would see me. The property did look creepy; there were no exposed windows, a few visible doors, but no real path to the house. So I made my own path. When I arrived at the back doorway, I walked into the house and looked around. There was an eerie feeling all around me, like something or someone didn't want me there.

Instead of turning around and leaving, I decided to look around. Just inside the back door was the kitchen. There was an old sink and an old crate stuffed with some newspapers from a long time ago. When I looked forward, there was a back-enclosed porch that led to a coal house where the coal was kept for heating. To the left there was the living room. Once in the living room, the first door on the left was a bedroom that circled around under the steps that led upstairs. After passing the steps, I was led into the living room. Up the stairway was a small room on the left, and to the right was another bedroom. Inside that bedroom was a small door that led to an attic that went above the living room.

The dangers inside the property were apparent. Sections of the living room were missing, so I had to be careful where I walked. I decided to leave my audio recorder on the steps, which seemed somewhat shielded by walls on both sides. I figured this would help minimize outside noises. Then I left for work. The recorder would be there the rest of the day.

When I got home later that day, I told my wife that I had left the recorder at the abandoned house and I had to go back and get it. She said she didn't mind, but I was blind to what her true feelings were: It was all about me and no one else. And she was right.

Later that night, I drove about 20 minutes from my house to the abandoned home. When I arrived there was a full moon. I could not ask for a more perfect setting. It was midnight, and I did not see any houselights turned on in the surrounding area. I admit that I was feeling a little scared about approaching the house in the dark because of the tall grass surrounding the property. The moon did shine into the home's windows though, adding to the mystery of the hunt.

I grabbed my camera, got up my courage, and ventured into the house. I retrieved my recorder from the steps and started videotaping throughout the house. I decided to go into one of the bedrooms, sit down in a corner, and ask the spirits to talk to me. I looked up and spotted birds' nests all around the room. I hoped I would not run into a bat.

I said aloud but very quietly, "Let me hear or feel your pain."

I did not get a response. In fact, everything was so quiet that I decided to leave about 45 minutes later.

When I got home, before going inside, I took a couple of snapshots of my house. In the first photo, there were no garage lights on; but, in the second one, the lights were on. Was it true that you could bring spirits back home with you? I didn't know the answer to this question, yet, but I would get my answer soon enough.

After taking a few photos, I went inside my house and began watching the video I took at the abandoned house. However, throughout the entire 45 minutes of video something had caused major static. However, the static seemed to only happen in response to my questions, almost like something was trying to answer me. I was impressed. There were more than 15 static responses immediately following my questions. I knew I had to go back to the location and try again. This strange electronic activity was only fueling my paranormal obsession, further arousing my curiosity and drive to know more about "the other side." Did an intelligent source cause the static? I had to find out.

It was a Saturday, and I didn't have to work, so I decided to listen to the audio from the old house. After listening for about two hours, I captured amazing audio of two male voices. This is what I captured:

"Give Anne a sedative!" a man yelled, while at the same time I could hear what sounded like a body (presumably Anne's) being shocked and then landing back on the box springs of a bed.

"One and a half?" the other man asked.

The audio took my breath away! I let my wife listen, and she said there could have been an ambulance in the area and that the recorder picked up their conversation. But I knew what it was. I had captured a residual imprint of an actual death happening at the location long ago.

As I listened more to the recording, I heard other conversations about taking a girl upstairs. And I captured the sound of a train going by. This was not an ordinary train. It had the sound of an old locomotive from the early days.

I discovered later that there used to be train tracks that ran 20 feet from the house. In the 1980s, they turned the old tracks into a bike trail. So, at the time of my recording, there were no trains nearby. This was a great discovery, and I was really excited to go back to the house that night.

I left around 11:30 p.m. and got there just before midnight. When I got back inside the house, I set the recorder on the floor in the living room by a trap door. I went into the kitchen and sat on a crate, waiting

40

and listening. I began asking questions like, "What is your name? How did you die? Why are you here?"

I never got a response, but as I listened, I heard footsteps in the living room leading upstairs. This actually scared me! I was hearing the footsteps with my own ears, and as soon as the footsteps stopped, the crate I was sitting on broke and I hit the floor! This was enough for me that night. I picked up my recorder and scooted quickly out the door.

Things that happened that night went beyond anything that had happened to me so far. I couldn't wait to tell someone about it. But, I decided to hold back. I had been talking to anyone who would listen to me about my investigations — talking all day, every day. It seemed like my entire world was being taken over by spirits.

I decided to take a few days off. Things were getting too crazy. I kept listening to the shocking of the body I had captured on my recorder. Could I have captured interference from an ambulance? I called the makers of the audio recorder I was using, but they said that it wouldn't pick up ambulances. It made my stomach flip to think it had to be very real!

Later that week I went back to the old house and was blown away when I saw the crate. It was in the bedroom, not in the kitchen, and it didn't have a scratch on it! It couldn't be. I broke it that night when I fell to the floor. Already things were getting creepy.

I set up in the living room this time, hoping I could film whatever was making the phantom footsteps. About half an hour went by, and I heard someone running around the house and then heading to the back door. I was really scared. Was there someone else in the house? But as the footsteps proceeded through the back door, the sound abruptly stopped. There was no one there! I felt like something or someone really wanted to connect with me.

I calmed myself down and walked over with my video camera to film the kitchen. I admit that I was scared, alone in a house late at night with no one to cover my back. I didn't stay much longer, and as I was leaving, I said, "Thank you."

What I heard in response still rings in my ears today.

"You are welcome," a disembodied voice answered.

I heard the words plain as day, like someone was talking directly to me.

The abandoned house (next to a barn) where I captured several EVPs and disembodied voices and noises.

What a way to end the night! I was excited to get back home to review the evidence. And when I finally arrived home, I got some coffee and started to watch the video, looking for anything strange and out of the ordinary. I did hear on the video footsteps running around, and I saw hundreds of strange sparkles in the footage. I believe these sparkles signified a spirit trying to manifest, and I didn't even realize it at the time!

As I listened to the audio the next day, I captured an EVP that said, "Anne." I decided to look on the Internet for any information about the property. I wanted to find out who owned it and who used to live there. It took some time, but I finally found what I was looking for. One of the first owners of the property was named Anne. As soon as I learned this information, I was positive Anne died in the home. I believed that medics probably tried to revive her at the house, and that is what my recording captured.

It was all making sense now. I went back to the house one more time, but not much happened. I did tell the spirit that I would be back the next weekend because my wife was going to stay at her parent's house. I planned on bringing some blankets back with me and staying the night. But I never did make it back. And I felt that whatever was there would not be happy with me for not returning as planned, so I actually stayed away for months and didn't go back. Something told me I wouldn't be welcome.

Chapter 10:
Halloween Hunt With a Local Radio Station

Summer was over, and it was almost time for Halloween. A local radio station wanted to hook up with some ghost hunters. I called in and talked to Puddin and his co-host, who were the morning radio hosts. They asked if I would show them a few haunted places.

We all met downtown on Halloween eve, and the station actually paid for two hearses to tag along with us, I guess to add to the excitement. It was so theatrical. We ended up having to fix one of the vehicles, because the muffler fell off on the way. Once we fixed the hearse, we were on the road again.

One of the hearses that local radio hosts rented for our paranormal investigation on Halloween night.

We ended up at Nunica Cemetery, which was well known for paranormal activity. Unfortunately, it was too windy and there were a lot of other people at the location doing the same thing we were. There would be little chance to do an investigation that was not tainted by others in the cemetery.

My Halloween investigation with the two local radio co-hosts turned out to be a bust!

So, I told the guys about the old, abandoned house that was only about 15 minutes away. We drove to the house and parked on the bike trail so no cars would see the hearses. There were about eight of us in total. As we went into the house, the station techs began recording the event for their morning show. They also took pictures and walked through the house.

"Let's go get the Ouija board and try to speak to the dead!" someone shouted out.

A woman from the show and several other attendees with us were anxious to play the game. One of the radio hosts emphatically stated that he did not want to touch the Ouija board.

I participated excitedly, happy to get another paranormal experience under my belt. I asked many questions during the Ouija board session. Something strange and very eerie happened every time a question was asked: The wind picked up, almost like it was responding to each question.

It was at about this time that we could hear the owners of the hearses throwing and breaking stuff inside the house. Suddenly, the window closest to one of the hearse owners blew out and glass flew everywhere. I felt that this event was not caused by the wind. Something had come through the Ouija board and released itself into the house, not happy about the destruction taking place inside.

We ended our Ouija session. I felt very bad that these guys were disturbing the house and not treating it with respect. I had brought them there. So I quickly planned a diversion and asked everyone to go check out the barn. Everyone went outside, but I stayed behind and headed upstairs to grab my recorder. When I returned downstairs, a door that was previously closed was wide open.

"Are you here with me?" I asked.

In response to my question, I heard a knock upstairs and captured three orbs on video, all different sizes heading toward the open door. Then, the door shut. There was no natural cause that could have closed the door. I was ecstatic that I captured all of this paranormal activity on my camera. I couldn't wait to share it with my friends and family!

This would not be my last night at the old house. I kept coming back. My time there was not finished.

Puddin and the rest of the crew wanted to go to another spooky location, as the night was still young. So we all got in the car and headed up toward Hell's Bridge. I knew how to get there, so I navigated the way.

There is an urban legend about Hell's Bridge. The story goes that many children were taken to the bridge and killed by an evil man. The legend also states that if you are at the bridge at midnight, you can hear the Devil speaking.

The bridge was right by the river, but to get there you had to walk a very long path. So I led a few of the radio crew members to the bridge, while Puddin stayed with a few others in the car.

The path we took to get to Hell's Bridge.

We arrived at the bridge, which was accentuated by a free-flowing creek. I walked over the bridge and recorded a few EVP sessions. Unfortunately, nothing of consequence occurred at the bridge that night. We all horsed around a bit and then decided to go back to the vehicles.

The location of Hell's Bridge where legend says you can hear the Devil speaking.

As we headed back into town, I realized it was around 4 a.m. My wife was going to kill me! She expected me home much earlier.

As we were riding back in one of the hearses, I listened to my audio again and heard a young girl say, "Help me!" Who the young girl was, I did not know. But I had a guess. Was she one of the children killed at the bridge? I began wondering if there was something more than just urban legend going on at Hell's Bridge.

As we arrived back at our meet-up point, I told Puddin the minute-mark where he could find the audio of the girl and handed him the audio recorder. I got into my car and headed home quickly. My wife was steaming when I arrived home, because I had to be up at 6 a.m. for work. Once again my paranormal obsession had led me astray.

49

As I got ready for work that morning, I listened to Puddin on the morning show. I was really excited when they amplified and played my audio of the little girl asking for help. Many people called in to discuss the recording. I decided to call in too. I wanted to share my excitement about this unexplainable voice I had captured just hours before. I was thankful the little girl communicated with me. I was also happy that others were able to hear the audio and share in something that I believed to be truly out of the ordinary.

I would like to thank this local radio show and its host, Puddin, for giving me a chance to get my story out on the radio.

Chapter 11:
Reconnecting With My Old Team

I found out that my old ghost-hunting team was adding investigation audio to their Website, so I decided to reconnect with them. I thought maybe this would give me the chance to share with others more of the amazing EVPs that I had collected. It seemed that the spirits continued to gravitate to my side and communicated with me often.

I was invited to attend a meeting at the team owner's house. When I arrived, I was surprised to see that hardly anyone else had shown up. It was a nice summer day, and I was wondering if I was wasting my time again, taking time away from my wife and children to attend to my obsession.

I filled the group in on the EVPs I had been collecting and how the recordings were getting better, perhaps even clearer, with each investigation. In fact, it seemed I could be just about anywhere and capture the voices of the dead on my recorder. During my research, I learned that I was getting a "direct connect" with the spirits, which means that I would ask a question during an EVP session and then get a specific answer from the spirit about themselves or the location.

The team immediately put me to the test, asking me to go inside the house and do a recording. I did as they requested, went inside, and proceeded to ask my usual questions. I captured an amazing EVP that night. I had been recording audio in the house and looking at a picture of Jesus on the wall when I captured this EVP: "Saint Peter, piece of me."

I believe spirits are everywhere, not just in "haunted" places, so I had no doubt that I could capture an EVP inside the owner's home even if it wasn't deemed "haunted" by anyone. But the review of the recording from that night would have to wait until the next day, because that night we decided to watch a few of my videos and discuss them.

As we watched the videos, I was somewhat concerned when many of the group members immediately said the activity I had captured could have been caused by anything. Even though the activity on the video happened on command, they discounted everything as being normal. Since they were a ghost group, I was confused as to why they didn't discuss both sides of the debate. Why did they instantly jump to a "logical" explanation and rule out the paranormal without more than a brief glance at the video?

I suggested, "If you have nowhere to go, let's head over to the house where it all happened."

Everyone agreed to go to the abandoned house. We met up at the town tavern with a few of the other team members who were running late. When we eventually got to the old house, the team owner and I went in first while everyone else stayed back. That first five minutes was very important, because we were catching the spirits off guard. I was pretty excited. I knew there would be some great EVPs captured that night.

When everyone else finally joined us inside, we sat in the kitchen and asked the spirits to give us some kind of sign of their presence. Nothing much seemed to happen that night; although, we did get some good pictures of interest.

The next evening I sent some of my EVPs captured at the abandoned house to the team's audio specialist. The spirits referred to "hiding around the corner" and "here we come." He reviewed the audio and got back with me, saying the voices I captured were the voices of some of the team's female members and not the voices of spirits.

The street leading to the old, abandoned house.

He was wrong. I knew the voices didn't belong to the living. How did I know? I had actually sent the audio specialist recordings of the owner and I in the abandoned house before the rest of the group had even joined us. There were no women in the vicinity of the audio recorder at the time.

By this time, several years had passed since my first investigation. I was getting very good at what I was doing, knowing how to eliminate potential contamination during an investigation. Unfortunately, the group did not seem to accept proof that was placed right in front of them. I again decided to end my relationship with this team.

Chapter 12:
A Haunted House Next Door

After the latest encounter with my old paranormal team, I realized I had to be on this journey alone. At least for now. So I started investigating by myself again. But I realized that I needed something more than just visiting that old home. I had to try something new. I soon found out that my new challenge was very close to home.

When I met my neighbors, they had been living on our street for more than two years. I decided not to hide my paranormal obsession from them and told them about my investigations and what I did. I expected them to think I was crazy. But, to my surprise, they told me there was something unusual and scary happening in their home. They said that their TV would turn on with no explanation, their children's toys would go on and off by themselves, and they heard disembodied footsteps and loud bangs and noises in the house. I immediately offered to help them find out what was going on.

Later that day, my neighbors invited me over, and I started recording as soon as I entered the house. I asked if I could go anywhere on the property, and they agreed. I walked through the kitchen first and asked my usual questions. When I proceeded into the children's bedroom, I felt that something was wrong, terribly wrong. In fact, as I stood there, I began to choke and my heart started to race. It felt as if a rope was hanging me. I soon began to feel the emotions of someone else, someone who was desperately attempting to try and stop what was happening to them.

I quickly left the room and walked back into the kitchen, revealing to my neighbors what had just happened. They looked at each other, exchanging bewildered glances. I would soon find out why they were so freaked out.

I completed my investigation of the home and then began listening to the audio with the neighbors. We soon heard something startling. I had actually captured a woman choking on the recording. I then revealed to the home owners that the EVP of the woman choking had been captured as I was going down to the basement earlier during the investigation.

It was at this time that the home owners revealed the secret of the house. They told me that the last owner took her own life by hanging herself inside the house in the basement. I could not believe that I had actually felt the woman's death and her heart racing during the last moments of her life. I realized that my emerging mediumistic abilities, which had begun erupting since my paranormal obsession began, were very real.

The joists where the former homeowner hung herself.

56

I told my wife, Anne, about what happened. I told her I had experienced many such psychic events since starting to investigate the paranormal. I told her I had a gift. But she didn't want to hear anything about it. I really wanted her to believe in me, and I needed her support. She was in denial about what was happening to me, and it pushed us farther apart.

That was not the last time I would visit my neighbors. One day they came over and told me they were having issues with the TV turning on and the toys talking when no one was playing with them, including a talking Teddy bear. I told my neighbors that the former home owner was most likely trying to reach them.

I took the Teddy bear from the neighbor's house and brought it back to my home. I set my audio and video recorders by the bear and began recording. Sure enough, it didn't take long for something to happen. What I call my "special hearing" kicked into gear, and when the bear talked, I could hear the ghost talking too. It was almost as if the spirit was reaching out through the stuffed animals and the toys.

And as if this haunting couldn't get any stranger, it did. The neighbors had a pet, a black cat. They claimed that the cat would say words in a growling sound during the night. They thought that the spirit was using the cat to communicate. I asked them if I could leave my recorder in their den and record the cat. They said yes, so one night I left the recorder at their house in an attempt to capture this unusual activity. I did indeed capture what seemed to be the cat growling "help" three separate times.

A couple of days later, the neighbors had a bon fire and I stopped over. They also had a friend over who was very religious. I had a talk with the friend about my paranormal investigations and research, and

I told her that I had many questions that were still unanswered. She said that she would set up a meeting for me with her pastor. I was happy to be put in touch with someone who could answer my questions.

As the night went on, I was able to convince the partygoers to let me record them. As a group, we all sat down together in each room of the neighbor's house. We asked specific questions like, "Who are you?" "Why are you here?" etc. Then we listened to the recorder … hearing several unidentified voices in the process. It seemed there was more than one spirit present. But the skeptical partygoers still weren't convinced. They had doubts. So, I showed them my Website, where I had posted some of my most unusual EVPs.

The EVPs blew their minds. If they could not make out the EVPs, I told them what I heard. Upon listening to the audio again, the group was impressed. I felt that my ability to clearly hear the spirits was a gift. And if others could not hear the voices, I would guide them through it until they could hear them too. I believe I helped them open their minds and senses to the possibilities. This night ended with a bang for me. I believe I made some believers out of good, religious people.

I was still interested in meeting with the friend's pastor, and the next day I went downtown and stopped by to talk to him. We went upstairs to his office, and I began to tell my story. But every time I revealed something to him, he moved backward in his chair. I really thought he was there to help, but I think that either he did not believe me and thought I was crazy or he did believe me but wanted no part of it. He was acting like I had a disease and he was going to get it too.

The pastor made a phone call to someone who he thought might be able to help me, and he gave me a few numbers to contact. But no one ever called me back. It seemed like there was always a dead end. No one wanted to help me. I think they all thought what I was doing was demonic or of the Devil. After this stage of my journey, I realized going the "church way" wouldn't help my situation. I felt a bit let down, but I wasn't going to let this roadblock stop me. I would find my answers another way.

After work that night, I arrived home a bit depressed. As I sat on my deck, I looked up at the sky and felt deep within myself that something strange was about to happen. The feeling was so strong that I had my video camera ready, just in case. Moments later I noticed something strange happening at my neighbor's house. Their lights were turning on and off. Was someone or something trying to signal me? It was late, and I didn't think anyone would be awake at that hour, so I put my video recorder on my deck and videotaped the neighbor's kitchen window for about five minutes.

I felt like I shouldn't be filming the house without permission, but at the same time I felt compelled to do so. My son awoke briefly, so I ran inside to put him back to bed. I then went back outside, grabbed the camera, and began to watch the recording. I couldn't believe my eyes! I had recorded my first shadow person.

As I started watching the video I had just filmed, I saw a glow cross the neighbor's kitchen window. I went inside and hooked the camera up to my TV and watched again as what looked like a small, solid black figure came into the camera frame very quickly. The figure seemed to look up at pictures on the wall, turn its head, and walk away. Was this the spirit of the former home owner who had hung herself? Or was it something else?

A minute later, my neighbor appeared on the tape, walking by the kitchen window and then walking back the other way again.

I could see where my obsession with ghosts was taking me. I was spying on my neighbors through their window in the hopes of catching ghostly activity. I woke my wife up and told her I had captured a shadow person on camera. Of course, she was not happy with what I had done. I can imagine how bad she must have felt.

The next day I decided to come clean with the neighbors. I invited my neighbor over to tell her what had happened and show her the video. Rather than being mad, she was frightened. She wouldn't go back inside the house until her husband came home. I made a copy of the tape for them and said I was sorry for filming their house without their permission but I had felt the spirits gave me a sign that something was going to happen. I told my neighbors that I would never do it again.

I felt bad that entire week, but my neighbors were showing the video to their friends and family, and no one could explain what they were seeing. From that point on, I did not film or record at their house. I decided to find someplace else to explore. My obsession was getting out of hand, but I couldn't stop. I had to find somewhere else to investigate.

Chapter 13:
The Haunted Roadside Cross & The Baby Graves

Things started to slow down again, until one day when I was driving home from work. I noticed a cross on the side of the road, a very big cross. I had driven that road hundreds of times and had never seen that cross before. I felt compelled to take a closer look at it.

I turned around and parked in front of the roadside cross, turned on my recorder, and started asking questions. On the cross was printed a first name, Ben, and 93 was the year the accident occurred. I sat for a few minutes recording. As I drove off, I listened to the audio. I was shocked at what I heard. The spirit had opened my car door, got in, and closed the door!

I said out loud, "I heard you get in and close the door."

*Did a spirit at this roadside cross hitch
a ride home with me?*

Wow was this really happening? I had read about spirits following people home before, but I thought they were extremely rare events. I knew right then that this would not be my last stop at the roadside cross.

A couple of days later, I had to go home the same way, so I stopped again and talked to who I thought was the spirit of Ben. I did not know his last name, but I did know the year he died. I told him if he was trying to reach someone to show me how to get more information about him.

Soon after, I had to leave to pick up my son at his cousin's house. As I was driving to pick him up, one of my coworkers called me for directions to his next job site. I pulled over into a cemetery to turn my computer on so that I could give him directions. As I finished, I looked up and was staring right at Ben's tombstone, the man from the cross that I had been researching. This had to be one of the biggest signs I had ever received. I needed information about him, and then I randomly ended up right in front of his tombstone? It was not a coincidence.

I feel I was led to this cemetery by the spirit of Ben.

I called my wife right away, really excited. But, still, it was not enough proof for her that something paranormal was going on. I was shot down again. It was hopeless to tell her anything anymore, but I still felt like I needed to try.

The graveyard was about three miles from my home, and I decided that it would be the next location that I would research. I was led there for a reason, and I had to find out why. Every night I began investigating the graveyard, hoping to understand why I'd been led there. I never made any contact with Ben's family. But there was still a reason I had to be there. So, I decided that I would put the time in with the hopes of getting some answers.

My video camera had broken again, so I only had my camera and audio recorder at this time. When I came back to the cemetery one night, I made sure that no one saw me going into the area. As I drove in, I spotted a figure playing around a tree. As I got closer to the figure, it ran to the right and out of view. I had seen my first ghost! While I was in awe at what I had seen, I was disappointed that I didn't have my video camera with me. But I still had my audio recorder to capture my excitement.

As I parked, I noticed the figure again! It looked like it was playing in the cemetery. I got out of my car and watched as the figure ran to the end of the graveyard, made a right turn, went down the graveyard road, and disappeared. I drove as fast as I could up to the spot where the figure had disappeared, and all I found was a grocery bag. Is that what I saw? A grocery bag? I could have sworn I had seen a ghostly figure. I was more confused than ever, not sure if my paranormal obsession was causing a lapse in my judgment.

Where I spotted the grocery bag flying through the air at the cemetery and what the grocery bag looked like.

I decided to leave my voice recorder at that spot, and then I left to borrow my sister-in-law's video camera. Once I had the video recorder in hand, I immediately returned to the cemetery to record. During my investigation that night, I captured something strange on video. I taped where I found the grocery bag, and in the background, it looked like a black figure "dropped" into the ground in front of a tombstone. Unfortunately, the camera did not have good night vision, so I decided to dismiss the footage as evidence.

Another interesting event captured my attention that night. At one point, I witnessed the grocery bag floating in the air and encircling a tree. When I went to investigate, I found two gravestones, one marked "Baby 1940" and the other marked "Irene May 4, 1906–May 25." The grocery bag was not floating very high off the ground, and it wasn't very windy that night, so I wondered if a child was controlling the bag and having fun running around the tree.

Another strange thing about the plastic bag — it was floating upside down the entire time. It seemed impossible for it to not spiral around if the wind was the cause of its movement.

While investigating a local cemetery, I was led to this spot.

The next day I listened to the audio of my investigation at the cemetery. I was shocked when I heard a voice say, "Irene." This was another direct connect that I had made! I also heard the sound of people walking on gravel, even though there was only grass around where I recorded.

As I looked back at some pictures taken, I was focused on orbs, wondering if they were paranormal in nature. My focus on the orbs caused me to miss something that my wife spotted when I showed her the photos. As she was browsing through the photos from the cemetery, she found an interesting picture. Sure it showed an orb, but what she saw above the orb was amazing. In the trees, she pointed out a child's face, so pure and so sweet. I never even saw the image, but she did.

My wife did not want to fuel my obsession even more, so she didn't make a big deal about the photos. She remained reserved about it.

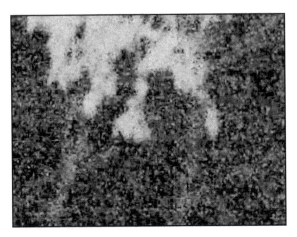

Do you see the child's face in the tree?

I went back to the cemetery a few more times because I believed that the little girl wanted to be noticed. And she was.

I want to point out one constant observation during my time at various cemeteries, including this one. While many individuals talk about how creepy and scary graveyards are at night, I found them to be quite peaceful.

Chapter 14:
Investigating My Own Home

My addiction was growing bigger and stronger than I ever thought possible. I eventually started bringing friends and family on ghost hunts with me, including to the cemetery. But it always seemed like I did not capture much evidence or have as many paranormal experiences when others were present. And I wasn't sure why.

I was so addicted to investigating that I started to research my own house. One night, I recorded a picture of my late mom and dad in the hope that something would happen. After an hour, I played the recording back, but nothing unusual was captured. I then recorded the pictures while asking my dad, if he was around, to knock twice, and if Mom was around to knock three times. When I listened to what I had recorded, I heard three knocks and a young female voice that said, "Be careful."

I shrugged off the message and continued investigating. I figured I was being as careful as I could. I started setting up my video camera and audio recorder each night, hoping something would make itself known. Nothing much happened until my wife bought an old toy from a yard sale. The toy held two small children swinging on wooden swings. It looked like it was at least 50 years old. So I decided to investigate the toy. I set it on my computer desk, put my audio recorder behind it, and set my video camera angled down toward the toy. I asked for some kind of connection from any spirits present, and then I went to bed.

When I awoke five hours later, I noticed that the video camera had fallen and landed on the floor overnight. I didn't have time to watch the footage, so I took it and my camera cord with me to charge on the way to work.

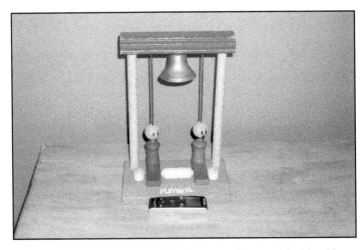

I conducted a spirit communication experiment with this old toy.

The battery was low, so I let it charge for about an hour. I was anxious to see if I captured what tipped over the video camera. Once the camera was charged, I realized that the recording was over an hour and a half long. And when I got to the point where the camera fell over, I realized that the camera has been slowly moving upward the entire time. In the hour and a half it was recording, the camera raised eight inches and then slowly started to fall. As it was falling, the camera turned from the "record" function to "play" and back to "record" when it hit the floor.

The small part that the video recorder played while it was falling was of my mom and dad's picture, as if they were trying to reach me. I tried to duplicate this event, but I could not. I added this video to my collection and until this day, I still can't get anyone to give me a good explanation about how it happened.

The room where the video camera fell to the floor.

My house started to become the center of my attention. If I was getting good results at home, why should I go out at night? It seemed like a waste of gas. So one night I thought I would go through every room of my house and try to get paranormal information. I started in the garage.

There was an old couch in the garage, and I sat down to rest my mind while trying to make contact with any spirits who might be present. I first asked the spirits to knock on my garage door. Lying on the couch, I filmed every moment. I then remembered being told that if you ask energy orbs to come to one of your hands, and it does, then it was indeed a spirit responding to your request. I made the request out loud and waited.

Later that night, I looked for anything paranormal on the footage. When I listened to the audio, at the point where I asked the spirit to knock on the garage door, I could hear a knocking happen right before I made the request. Could the spirits read my thoughts even though they weren't voiced yet?

Next, when I got to the point on the tape where I raised my hand and asked a spirit to go through it, I could see a small orb come from my body, go up to my hand, and then quickly turn left and change shapes as it went out of sight.

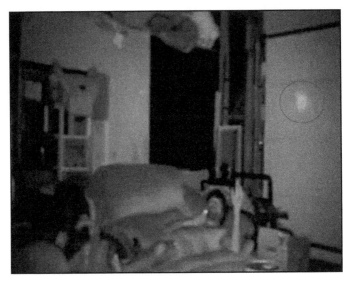

The orb circled in red materialized on command.
(Screen capture from video.)

These experiences continued to fuel my paranormal obsession. I kept thinking about all the mysteries out there that no one has even come close to tapping into. It seemed like the more I practiced paranormal investigation at home, the more experiences came my way. It became obvious to me that the spirits around me were taking over my life. I was not blind to my obsession, which had only just begun.

One day, I was doing laundry in my basement and the light turned on and off on its own. As I began to ask questions, the light turned on and off in response. I retrieved my video camera, called my son down, and asked him to ask the spirit to turn the light off. My son then asked the spirit to turn the light off, and it did.

I wondered if I had brought spirits home with me from my previous investigations. Did they actually hop in my car and take a ride with me, almost like ghostly hitchhikers? I had previously heard one spirit open my car door, after all.

Sometimes I could feel the spirits and hear them; even my dogs reacted to them. My dog would bark in every room, letting me know that something was moving through the house.

One night while at home, I began hearing strange noises coming from my attic over my head. I had never heard anything like it in my 14 years of living there. I admit that I got scared. I ended up calling my sister, Joyce, in Kentucky, and asked her to say a prayer for me. As she was praying, I began to hear noises in my attic. This really freaked me out, because it had never happened before.

That night when I went to bed, I left my audio recorder on the TV stand. I tried to sleep, but I couldn't. And at one point during the night, I felt something climbing up my covers! My body went stiff as extreme fear gripped my soul. I felt goose bumps on my head. I knew something was there. Whatever it was finally stopped moving, so I grabbed the recorder. I played it back and was immediately stricken with fear again. I heard what I can only describe as evil growling sounds coming through the recorder, along with a voice that said, "We want him."

I realized that I had a negative spirit in my home. Did I cause this to happen by bringing home spirits with me after my paranormal investigations? Or did I open myself up to the activity because I was investigating my own home?

I hopped on the Internet the next day and told my story on a Website dedicated to the paranormal. One person told me to say the Lord's Prayer and make a sign of the cross over every window. They told me that then the spirit would not come back into the house. I did what she said and noticed an immediate change in my dog; she took a break from barking.

A couple of days passed, and I still wondered if that really happened. At times, I tried to look the other way, but no matter where I looked, it was coming straight at me.

Chapter 15:
My Sister-in-Law's Home

One evening, our family set out to have dinner at my sister-in-law Shell's house. When we arrived, my son went into her basement to play. Ten minutes later he ran upstairs saying something scared him. I quickly grabbed my camera and went downstairs.

I asked my son to take me to where he was playing in the basement. He led me to the back room where he pointed and said, "There Daddy."

I took five pictures of the area, and out of the five photos, one was unusual. It showed nothing but blackness. Once we arrived back home, I loaded the pictures onto my computer. I wanted to see if I could determine what was in the blackened-out photo. And, sure enough, when I lightened it up, I saw a figure standing in front of my son, who was pointing right at the figure as it was facing him! The figure looked taller than my son and had a complete form, including arms and legs (see picture on the next page).

I began putting my pictures and videos on Ghostplace.com. I tried to uncover what was really on the videos and in the pictures by reaching out to others, and boy, did I have fun. Some people were amazed, while others were doubters who had some weird explanations for the phenomena. I had so much strange audio, video, and photos that some people thought it was all phony. I can tell you from my own experiences that none of it was fake.

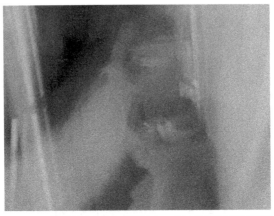

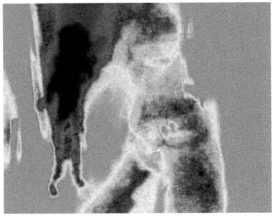

Pictured at top: The lightened photo of my son pointing at an entity in the basement of my sister-in-law's home. The next photo is an adjustment of the original photo.

I replayed the scene for people so they could see the surrounding area and make a better judgment. My efforts seemed to prove to some that I was genuine, because people saw I was making every effort to prove that what I had recorded was real. However, with others, it didn't make a difference, because no matter how much research a person puts out there, some people's belief systems just won't let them believe in something outside of their comprehension.

After the picture in the basement, I was determined to investigate my sister-in-law's house. Shell went up north that weekend and said I could investigate her house. I was anxious to do that investigation after the picture of my son and the strange figure. That night I set my audio recorder in the house and left it overnight. Upon reviewing the audio the next day, at about 1 a.m., I heard a door shut. Then at about 3 a.m., I heard someone walking down the steps past my recorder. It ran through the living room to the back door and then shut the door.

I captured what sounded like spirit children running up and down the stairs at my sister-in-law's house.

No one was home at the time and, to me, this was excellent proof that something paranormal was taking place at the house. Whoever was running was also talking. It sounded like a child giggling and laughing as they ran down the stairs.

But my wife and sister said it was probably the neighbor kids breaking into the house. Based on their response, I decided to conduct an experiment. I put the recorder back where it was and hollered in three different areas, one inside the house and two outside. The only one that sounded like the previous recording was the one inside the house.

The next time I tried recording again, I took a picture of the recorder's position. When I came back a couple of hours later, it had been moved. As I listened to the audio, it sounded like something was playing with the recorder, but no one was in the house at the time. Later on in the audio, it sounded like an old man yawned. It was very clear, so I let my sister-in-law listen. She was clearly puzzled at what she heard.

I decided to leave my audio recorder in each room of the house to see what I could capture. I first put it in the office while we all went to the park. When we returned to listen to the recording, we heard a person singing a song that no one knew. It must have been an old song. And in the basement, I captured a small child saying, "Help me." I could also make out an older person talking.

It was time to do some research on the history of the house, so I went to the library and looked up the address. I found names of some of the former owners of the house, but there wasn't much helpful information. A neighbor, who was over 100 years old, told my sister-in-law about how the old lady who lived there got sick, but would not come out of the house. I believe it was because one of her sons never returned from World War II.

I conducted another experiment by lying on a bed in one of the bedrooms and asking for the female or male spirits to come and talk to me. After a bit I dozed off, and when I woke up I felt a soft touch going over my leg — enough to raise the hair on my arms, as well as my fear.

It seemed like everywhere I went strange happenings took place. I was getting so much activity that I thought I would check out some new ghost-hunting groups. As I was looking at teams in my surrounding area, I found my old group that had regrouped with different people. It looked like they had gotten rid of the troublemakers and actually looked a bit more professional. They were seeking some haunted locations to investigate, so I contacted them about investigating Shell's house. They said yes, and Shell agreed on a date and time. However, she decided she didn't want to be present during the investigation.

My sister-in-law's house where paranormal activity occurred frequently.

It was around 7 p.m. when we all met at Shell's house. It was a nice evening, and everyone was excited. We did our usual thing by letting one medium go through the house first as we video and audiotaped her experiences. Then the second medium did the same thing as we recorded her experiences. Finally, we all gathered together outside to talk about what happened. The first medium told a story about a man upstairs and in the kitchen. The second medium talked about an old woman upset in the basement.

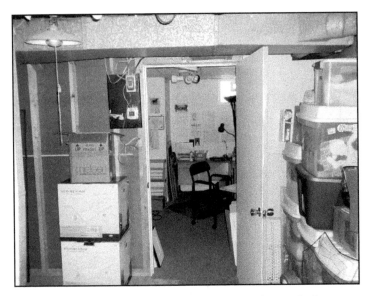

The basement where part of the investigation took place.

Based on this information, we all got together and hit these two spots first. We went to the basement and sat on the floor. One medium asked questions, hoping for a response. We all listened and videotaped the session. A bit later, one of the team members pulled out a pendulum and tried to communicate with the spirits that way. It did seem like something was affecting the pendulum.

After trying to communicate in the basement, we went upstairs to the master bedroom. This seemed to me like a very active room. In this room, Shell had seen a military man standing in the corner. It was also where I felt something stroking my leg. While we were in the room, one of the mediums talked about a spirit slowly rubbing across a person's leg. I said that was exactly what happened to me. It was strange how she picked that up. It was as if she was seeing it happen in front of her. It was hard to believe, but I could verify everything she was saying because it happened to me personally. The medium

78

kept mentioning a female's name, Clarisse. Of course, I was recording every minute. Through my research, I already knew things about the house, even though the group did not. I had something to compare it with when they were done investigating.

Next we decided to go into the room farthest back, the bedroom. This room also proved to be extremely active. The mediums continued to see an old lady in the basement and a soldier coming back from the war in spirit. When we finished with the investigation upstairs, we decided to have a séance in the dining room. I videotaped the session from the fireplace, zooming in so I would see any movement or strange occurrences.

Nothing of consequence occurred during the séance, so another team member and I decided to go back to the basement. We went down and asked a few more question and took a few more pictures, but we had to end our night because Shell returned home. The team thanked Shell and said they would get back with me after reviewing their evidence.

When I reviewed my own evidence, I heard a female voice responding by saying her name when one of the mediums asked if the spirit of Clarisse was present. In the basement, I captured a large black orb shooting in front of us. And then in the living room, there was a big flash when we were ready to go down to the basement. It was not caused by a camera. The mediums had mentioned a young military man coming home from the war in spirit, and from the research I did I knew that the son of one of the former home owners was killed during the war.

At this point, my paranormal fascination had an even tighter grip on my psyche. I needed another home to investigate, so I set my sights on my mother-in-law Ava's home. Her home had burned down once before and was later rebuilt on some of the old foundation. I figured that any memories of the past would still be present.

I first started recording when no one was in the house. But first I decided to conduct a brief experiment. I put the audio recorder on her China cabinet and made a drum beat seven times. I then went upstairs to use the restroom. When I returned downstairs, I listened to the brief recording and heard the exact same drum beat. Strangely enough, I also heard a rooster crow as if it was right there inside a coop.

The China cabinet where I heard the drum beat.

I wondered if the old owners, who had died on the property, were responsible for the responding drum beat or if it might have been my wife's deceased grandmother. I played the recording for my father-in-law Mike. While he said it sounded cool, it didn't mean much to him. Others listened to the recording as well, but no one seemed interested in it.

Chapter 16:
Ghostly Breathing

It wasn't a big secret with my family and friends that I investigated any home I could find. So, one day, my father-in-law told me about an old, abandoned house back by the woods on his neighbor's property. The family used to take walks over there when their kids were little. Of course, I had to go and check it out.

That night I gathered my equipment and went to the house next to my in-laws. When I arrived there was a full moon. It was so bright that I could walk through the fields without a flashlight. I went through the side door of the abandoned home and sat on some old boards. I set my camera and the audio up, and then I began to take pictures. I had been there for about 10 minutes, when I started to hear something strange. It sounded like heavy breathing.

I captured what sounded like heavy breathing at this abandoned house.

I had previously been told that if you hear breathing from an unidentifiable source during a paranormal investigation it was not a good thing. So, I began to get a bit nervous. Then I heard something moving in the corner. I listened intently on the breathing, and it was so clear that it sounded like it was right in front of me.

"Can I help you move on?" I asked.

There was no response. So I talked for a little while longer, and each time I asked a question, I would hear breathing in response.

I ended up rushing back to my in-law's house to look up some things on the computer. But something so startling happened when I arrived home, that I will never forget it. I heard breathing coming from behind me. It was then that I realized whatever was in the abandoned house followed me home!

A spirit seemingly followed me from an abandoned house to my in-law's home.

I didn't stay up much later that night, because I was very tired. But before heading to bed, I put the recorder on the counter and started recording. I thought maybe the spirit that followed me might talk on the recorder.

The next day was a good day. I knew what happened the night before was exceptional. When I told my family about all that had happened, they told me that it was most likely an animal breathing and not a ghost. I took in what they said, but deep down inside I knew it wasn't an animal. I then began listening to my audio from the night before at my in-law's house. I heard someone in the kitchen making an awful noise slamming doors, moving things, and walking around loudly. I even heard what sounded like a woman taking her last breath. I wondered if this person could have been one of the former home owners who lived and died on the property.

When I asked my mother-in-law if anyone was in the kitchen the night before, she said no, but that her house makes noises all the time. When I let her hear the recording, the activity recorded surprised her, as well as how loud it was. I was excited about the recording, but no one else seemed to really think much of it.

The next evening I left the audio recorder in the basement when we all left to visit a relative. When we returned later that night, I retrieved the recorder and began listening. What was interesting was that I captured a conversation between two women talking about going to the garden. It was amazing to hear a beautiful conversation from the past. They mentioned fruits and vegetables and how the garden was growing.

I felt that this evidence was another piece of my paranormal puzzle. And it added fuel to my search for answers about life after death.

My in-law's basement where I captured an EVP of two women talking about going to the garden.

Chapter 17:
Trying to Break the Obsession

Since I first began investigating the paranormal, I knew there was a purpose for it, even though I didn't know exactly what was to come later in my life. And now, after experiencing so much paranormal activity, I knew I couldn't stop investigating. So, I set out to capture even more evidence of the afterlife.

I started to test the spirits by putting flour on my floor at home — hoping to get a footprint — and setting out toys for child spirits to play with. Then I set up video and audio recorders to collect the responses. I did everything I could to capture any responses to my attempts at communicating with the spirits.

I also tried to find people to talk to about my experiences, but no one was interested. Some people would listen to me, but they oftentimes denied there was anything paranormal going on and certainly did not want to participate in what I was doing. At one point, as a result of the reactions I was getting from people when I shared my research and experiences with them, I began questioning my mental state. So I called several mental healthcare facilities to see if they had any specialists who I could talk to. But they wouldn't give me the time of day, other than wanting to admit me to their facilities.

I even contacted American Indian reservations to try and find someone to talk to about spirit activity. But they referred me back to the mental health professionals. Not many people seemed to believe what I was hearing and feeling, and my wife was getting increasingly upset with me as well.

While I felt like I had to go on with my daily life of feeling and hearing spirits, I was frustrated. So, I eventually decided to take a break from using my equipment.

In fact, the night before my wife's birthday, I got the bright idea that I would record myself breaking my audio recorder. It really took a lot of courage for me to break that recorder. Everything inside me told me not to do it. But I went through with it anyway. And when I woke up the next day, I was extremely unhappy with what I had done.

Regardless, I gave my wife the video of me smashing my audio recorder that I was so addicted to. She couldn't believe what I'd done. Her parents were present, and I apologized for not understanding her needs and feelings. I meant what I said, but not very long after my wife's birthday, I started feeling like I needed that audio recorder back. I just could not function without it, and I was getting depressed. Whatever was happening to me, I knew I had to get another recorder.

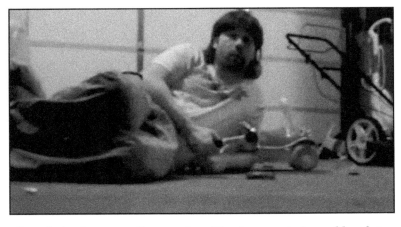

I am destroying my audio recorder with a hammer to try and break my paranormal obsession. (Screen capture from video.)

One day while we were out shopping, I slipped a brand new recorder and some rechargeable batteries into our cart. I asked my wife to take the kids to the car and told her that I would pay for everything and meet them there. She never knew I had bought a new recorder. My paranormal obsession had, again, led me to do something sneaky. I took the receipt and threw it away. I also started to blatantly lie to my wife each day, hiding any paranormal research I was doing.

I could see how happy she was that I did not have a recorder. And I wanted to keep seeing her happy, which is why I lied. And when I would go to bed at night, I would pray for God to bless me with more psychic gifts.

Chapter 18:
My Struggle to Find Answers

With my paranormal obsession back in full swing, I decided to create a new Website so that I could share my evidence with others. I included all my recordings and photos that I had gathered over the years. I thought that if I could put everything out there, someone would take notice and possibly want to try and help figure things out. But months later, while I had many site visitors, no one had even responded. What did I have to do to get someone to notice?

I figured that I would get proactive and contacted some paranormal investigators who appeared on a popular TV show. I also sent them a lot of my evidence. But I never got a call or email in response. I felt like I was cursed and that no one would help me.

At this point, I started investigating at my home again, setting up tests in my basement. One experiment included water, a golf ball, and some paper and pen. I hoped that the spirits would write on the paper, spill the water, or move the ball, but nothing happened. It felt almost like the spirits were getting upset with me because I could not get anyone of importance to listen to my story.

One day, I called Notre Dame College and talked to a psychology professor about what was happening to me. We had discussed recording an EVP session during his class and then playing back the audio and listening for spirit communication in real time. He asked me to meet with him and some of his students the following Wednesday. He also told me to call on Monday to confirm. Monday came, and I called to confirm. The professor said he had to cancel our meeting. Here we go again! Another person scared of what might happen to them if they got involved in paranormal investigation. Another dead end. No matter where I went, there were roadblocks. It was like something did not want me to go public. Were my Angels guarding me from something? Whatever was happening to me, I needed to find out why it was happening.

Over time, it seemed like my experiences with the spirits were turning darker. For instance, one spirit would tell me, "Sally killed me," and the next night, "John did it." Then, "Thomas was the one."

I started to get frustrated, even angry, so I gave up recording audio for awhile. But the spirits did not stop communicating with me. One day I ventured into an old house in town. No one was there, but I kept hearing a whistling song. That entire day things were happening. At a customer's house that day, I sensed that a loud bang was about to happen. In fact, I was so certain that I told the customer something was about to happen, and right then it sounded as if a truck hit her home. We both went outside, but there was nothing there.

The old home in town that I ventured into.

90

The next week I still was not using the recorder. I was at customer's home getting ready to measure another basement. As soon as the customer started to go upstairs, all of the basement lights started going off and on repeatedly.

"Has this ever happened before?" I asked her.

"No," she answered.

At another customer's home, the closet door slammed shut in front of us. More paranormal events were happening, and it was getting to the point where others were hearing and seeing the paranormal activity as well.

One day I was downtown and my customer told me he was scared of his house.

"Weird things are happening," he told me.

I was working on his kitchen at the time, and he was standing next to me, and as I walked toward his closet, a loud bang hit the door from the inside. My customer looked at me with fear. I suggested that he contact a paranormal group in the area to see if they could help him.

No matter what I was doing or who I was with, it seemed that someone was always trying to make contact with me. That night we had a bad storm, and a wire fell on the ground, hitting our circuit breaker and frying our computer hard drive. I lost hundreds of EVPs and most of my work for the past two years. It was all gone, and I was very upset.

I continued to research spirit activity and read as many books as I could find on the paranormal. I found out that throughout history, there have always been people claiming to experience the same types of phenomena I was experiencing. I also found a Website that allowed member to post their EVPs, and other members would

91

comment on them. I was excited to get started, but I had lost almost everything I had recorded. Then I remembered that I had shared some of my EVPs online, so I was in luck.

I ended up retrieving some of my audio from the various Websites where I had previously uploaded them to and then posted them on the new site I found. I did start hearing back from people, but it seemed that many of them could not clearly hear the EVPs. I began listening to some of their EVPs, and I could not hear what they were hearing. I spoke to the owner of the Website, who told me that an EVP has different class types: A, B, and C. She told me I was getting Class C EVPs. She explained it like this: If 10 people listened to my audio and 10 people said they heard the same thing, it is a Class A EVP, which is very rare to find. She sent me a Class A EVP, and sure enough, I heard the same thing that everyone else heard.

I began to wonder, though, if some spirits talked to some people in different ways. Maybe there was a reason that people heard different messages from the same EVP. Maybe the spirits talk to each person in their own way.

Even though I was confused about the extreme differences in people's perceptions of EVPs, I still believed in the gifts that I had. I had talked to many people with similar talents, and they said that their gifts evolved in ways they didn't seem to have control over. This was both exciting and scary.

Chapter 19:
The Paranormal Conference

More time passed on my paranormal journey. I continued researching and investigating. One weekend I was browsing the Internet and discovered there was a ghost-hunting expo taking place in Allegan, Michigan. It looked like the event would be a great place to meet other mediums and investigators. Of course, it would cost a little money, but my wife and I decided to book the conference.

We were both excited about it. My wife wanted to get some answers about her friend who had been murdered, and I wanted any information I could get access to. The conference took place at a local church, and when we walked in, there was a long sign-in table where they handed out programs. The first speaker was one of the hosts, and she talked about her life, why she got into the paranormal, and the benefits of joining a paranormal a team. She also discussed her training in past-life regression and asked everyone in attendance to try it right then and there.

We all closed our eyes, and she began to count backwards. We were all supposed to think of something from our childhood that made us feel good. She talked about the ocean and took us back to when we were young kids. And then back to when we were one, back to when we were in the womb, and even further back. She then started bringing us back through the stages until we were back in the room. I did not get much out of this, but something did happen. During the regression I saw myself alone in the desert with sand all around me. I wasn't sure what it meant, but it was interesting nonetheless.

After the regression session, we all took a break. My wife and I went outside and got a reading from a medium. We paid $40, and she read both of us. We were a bit disappointed with the reading, because while the medium did hit on some things that seemed to relate to us, most of what she said did not make sense.

The church where the paranormal conference took place.

After half an hour, we were back inside. Next up, a medium went from person to person trying to do quick reads. One woman began crying after the medium hit on a name that no one would have known. Then she came over and started reading my wife. She said that my wife had lost a friend in a car crash, which was wrong. She was actually killed by a jealous boyfriend. The more the medium said, the more my wife lost interest.

Then she turned to me. I was excited to see if she could pick up on what was going on with me, but her reading started wrong and ended wrong.

Next up we listened to other speakers talk about their paranormal journeys. One speaker showed us how to put paper over a candle, move it around, and look for a picture that revealed something about our lives or our angels. I ended up getting something strange, but my wife got a heart shape. I wasn't really impressed with the exercise.

After our lunch break, we headed back to the church, but we started wondering if the conference was worth it. When we arrived back at the meeting room, Kathy Conder, founder of the paranormal group holding the conference, wanted me to record in the church where they were going to hold their ghost hunt that night. I agreed to record and went into the church with Kathy. I instantly felt something run through my body, almost like something was either trying to greet me or run away from me. I recorded for almost 15 minutes and then went back into the conference.

Upon returning, a medium was reading people again. Then Kathy presented her story to everyone in attendance. She told us about her childhood when she discovered she had a gift. She had a vision of a dead relative, and after doing some research, she discovered that some of her ancestors had the same gift. Kathy seemed like a person I could work with.

After our next break, I paid a Taro card reader $20. She did a read on me, but nothing matched. Another disappointment.

That night at dinner break, my wife was tired, so she took a nap while I went into a graveyard and listened to my audio from the church. Incredibly, I had captured 20 EVPs. I gave my list of EVPs to Kathy when we returned to the conference for the last session.

The final speaker was a police officer and a medium. Her story was that one day, out of the blue, she started drawing pictures of people and things. They didn't make much sense to her until she read on the news about a murder in the next county. She looked at her picture and, sure enough, her drawing was a picture of the murderer. At that moment, she knew she was on a new journey.

Finally, it was time for some fun, so we divided into teams to solve a murder. But before we all started, we had to take a "psychic test." First, we had to guess a color that would soon appear. I said blue. It was blue. The next test was to predict the next word that would come up. I saw in my mind the color red and heard the word red. Red was the word. The next thing was to guess a number. I could see the number six when I closed my eyes, and sure enough it was a six. The last question I missed, but three out of four was not bad! My wife didn't fare as well and missed all of her predictions.

We were excited to finally start our murder/mystery game. Although, in this version of the game, we worked with our "spirit guides" to find answers. Each team was asked to focus on different parts of the fictional murder. For instance, one group was handed objects that might have killed the victim, while another group was given a picture with several criminals, including the killer. In the end, we all predicted the killer, what he was wearing, and how he killed the victim. It was a very fun ending to the conference.

While I felt it was a great night, my wife did not. She told me she would never waste her time on such stupid research ever again. I was disappointed that she did not find the experience valuable, as I felt that I personally walked away with a very different perspective on the things around me.

I had recorded the entire day at the conference and ended up capturing many EVPs and disembodied voices, including during the regressions when no one else was supposed to be speaking.

It was at this point in my journey that I began to truly fall in love with paranormal research and the investigation process, especially when adding psychic abilities into the mix.

Chapter 20:
Hiring an Employee

I was getting ready to start looking for a new employee to help me at work, because I needed someone to help with my workload. As I was about to put an ad in the paper, I got a call from my sister. She said she had a friend looking for some work. So, I said I would call her and set up an interview.

One thing that my friends and family know about me — I have a big heart and always want to help everyone. And this time was no exception. I met with my sister's friend, Jan, and as we talked I instantly picked up on a spirit around us. I held my tongue and didn't say anything about what I was sensing.

I ultimately made Jan a job offer, and she said yes. Her first day went well, but I wasn't sure if she was a perfect fit for the job yet. However, she was definitely a hard worker and trying her best. The next time we spoke, I couldn't restrain myself any longer. I told her about my paranormal investigations.

Jan was surprised about my admission yet very interested at the same time, as her husband had passed away the year before.

Unfortunately for Jan, once I had her willing ear, I began revealing everything about the paranormal journey I had been on. But she was quite nice about it and listened politely. I told her about how almost every time I would enter a home, I would feel the spirits go through me, pretty much taking my breath away. In fact, sometimes they would take all my energy, and I would need to step out of the situation to get my energy back.

It wasn't long before we were recording in my car, and this time she said one of the voices captured sounded just like her sister. The next week, she got a call that her sister had died in an accident. I asked my employee if she wanted me to go to the accident site and record audio, and she said yes. I conducted the session and captured the following recording: "She was hit from behind and killed."

I heard that same wording 10 more times on the recording. I had never had a voice repeat itself that much in the past.

One morning, we were sitting in the car waiting for a customer to arrive. We were recording an EVP session while we waited, and when we played it back, I heard something on the recorder.

It sounded like Jan's mom was complaining about the toaster not working. Jan revealed earlier that very morning, before she met up with me for work, she was at her mom's house. While there, her mom was talking about the toaster not working and that she was going to buy a new one. From that point on, my new employee was very interested in what I had to say.

In fact, we decided to record at her house and see what we could capture. By the end of the night, we had picked up some paranormal activity, but not as much as I usually captured when investigating alone. When I got home that night, I loaded my recordings onto my computer. When listening back, it seemed that I had made contact with a spirit. I heard what sounded like a zipper and a man complaining about not getting his chickens; his voice seemed to be weak, and his name sounded familiar.

When I talked again with my employee, I shared with her what I had captured. She told me a story about how her husband would always zip up his boots every morning and that she still could hear it in her head. She also told me the story about how, one day, her husband came home with a truckload of chickens. She turned him away at the door, telling him there was no way he was going to bring those chickens in the house. She said he was so mad about those "damn chickens." Neither of us could make anything out of the name on the recorder, however.

About a week later, Jan told me her mother was in bad shape and did not have much time to live. A few days later, her mother passed on. Jan's mom died two weeks after her sister. This was really shocking. And I began wondering, *Am I the Grim Reaper or what?*

My employee decided to take time off from work indefinitely. She was extremely stressed out by the deaths in her family and felt she could not perform her duties. Before she left, I gave her a name I had captured on the recorder. When she attended her mother's funeral, she met an old friend from many years ago. Sure enough his name was the one I had captured on the recorder.

I took my audio recorder with me everywhere to try and record spirit voices.

Chapter 21:
Phantom Trains Captured at an Abandoned School

One morning my wife and I were driving to a job site, and I spotted an abandoned school on the way. I asked her if I could stop and put my audio recorder in the doorway. She agreed. Stopping, I got out of my vehicle and approached the school house. When I got to the old, beat-up door, I asked the spirits to please come and communicate by talking into the recorder, and then I laid the recorder inside of the door.

I got back into my car and drove 20 minutes to my job site. When my wife and I finished at my jobsite that day, we went back to the school. I retrieved my recorder from the school house, thanked the spirits, and headed home. As we drove home, I began listening to the audio I had captured. Immediately, I heard many sounds I was not expecting. I was amazed when I heard a train going by, and then a few minutes later I heard another train.

I handed the recorder to my wife so that she could listen to the audio, and she also heard several trains on the recording. The strange part about the recording was that there were no trains within 20 miles of the abandoned school. Even my wife, ever the skeptic, was puzzled with all the trains rolling by on the audio.

Later that night, I did some research on old school houses and train stations in the area, and I uncovered an interesting historical fact. There used to be a train depot 30 miles from the school house, but it was eventually dismantled. They reportedly used the old bricks from the train station to fix up several schools around the area.

I believe what I captured on the audio were phantom trains. Why? Because the bricks transported from the train station to the school contained residual energy of events that had happened in and around the station.

I listened to more of the audio and heard what sounded like individuals getting on and off the trains and walking away. I heard what sounded like workers doing their jobs, and many footsteps were also recorded.

The next time I came by that way, I asked a neighbor by the school if they knew who owned the property. The man told me that he was the owner. I asked him if he could give me more information about the property and if I could investigate it. But he told me that he was going to tear it down because it was a hazard. I said OK and moved on my way.

The place never did get torn down, and it still stands today.

The abandoned school where I caught phantom trains on
my audio recorder.

Chapter 22:
Barbara The Gray Witch

One day while working, I heard a local radio station interviewing Barbara the Gray Witch. She was discussing spirit contact and similar subjects. I wrote down her number and left her a message. She called me back that day, and we chatted for some time. We decided to meet to share information and research her home.

We met at her house the following Friday around noon, as we were going to have lunch before investigating. The house was very cool and really creepy. It was like going into a haunted house. As soon as I got to the porch, I started recording. She took me through the house, telling me stories about the history of the property and the previous owners. Barbara even revealed a murder that had taken place in the basement when a previous owner had lived in the home. The victim had been cut up in the basement.

The house of Barbara the Gray Witch.

As we walked upstairs, there was a picture on the wall of the Fox sisters, who played an important role in the Spiritualist movement. She also showed me a door upstairs that would slam shut all the time. Was her story believable? I did not know, but I was excited to investigate. And the more I opened myself up to the possibilities, the more exciting my journey was getting.

We put a recorder in an active location, and then decided to talk for a bit. So, I went back to the kitchen and sat with Barbara. We drank some coffee and chatted about the place, and before we were done, I could hear a sound coming from the basement. Barbara could hear it too, so she told "it" to be quiet. The noise stopped. I asked if I could check the noise out myself, and she said OK. As soon as I walked by the steps, I heard what sounded like children running up the steps.

That day, it seemed something unusual happened in every room. As I was going upstairs, I heard the door slam exactly as Barbara had said it did so often. No doubt in my mind; this place had it going on. But the atmosphere made the visit way better than any other place I had been in before. She even had a séance table and a casket. How she talked to the spirits was amazing, and the spirits listened. I never thought this type of in-your-face activity was possible, but my eyes started to open more and more with every experience.

When we were done investigating, I picked up my recorder and thanked Barbara. As I drove off, I looked at the cool, old house with ravens on top. That night I did my usual thing and listened to the audio. It turned out that upon my arrival at the property, a spirit woman invited me in. And the recorder picked up lots of children, the shutting of the door, and what sounded like the murder victim being cut up in the basement. Everything Barbara had mentioned proved itself to me during that one visit.

After this experience, my paranormal obsession began to lessen a bit. I felt I had some answers, and my intense drive to continually record audio to try and capture spirit voices began to dull. I found myself "listening" to audio less and less. My wife still wasn't happy with my investigations, but she was realizing it was not as much of a priority in my life as it had been.

I wasn't done investigating by a long shot. In fact, I went to work one morning and decided to try something new. I would begin to test my psychic abilities.

Barbara had a séance table and a casket in her home.

Chapter 23:
Seeing Things

I was getting to a point where the audio recorder obsession was finally lessening. But, I wasn't done quite yet. I decided to record at my next customer's home. But before arriving, I visualized the house in my mind. Right away, in my mind's eye, I saw a very colorful bed in a corner. The covers were pulled over, and the sheet was tucked around covering the blanket.

I soon arrived at the house and started my job measuring the rooms. When I got to the last room, there was a bed in the corner exactly as it had been in my mind's eye. This really took me by surprise. What was happening to me? Was my mind opening up even more to psychic possibilities based on my paranormal investigations?

I thought I would try visualizing my next home. When I did, I saw an open *Bible*, a lot of shoes, a pair of brown boots, a red wall, and a heart on a shirt. When I arrived at my client's home, I did not see any of the items that I had visualized. I wondered how I could have been so off ... until it all started falling in place. I opened one of the home's closet doors and spotted an open *Bible* and a lot of shoes.

The homeowner then came in, and he had a heart on his shirt. As I was leaving, I also saw a big, red wall. I did look for the brown boots, but didn't see them. However, as I was walking out, the homeowner said she needed to take the dog out, and she reached behind the couch and pulled out the brown boots!

After this day, I believed I had found my next gift, one I needed to pay attention to. I started calling family members to tell them what had happened, and they were impressed. So I started "reading" them.

As I was talking to my sister-in-law in Ohio, I told her I saw running water by her. She said she was looking at a fish tank right at that moment. She said it had a water line with running water.

I began psychically tuning into remote locations,
including my sister-in-law's house.

Next, I told her that I could see a leather jacket. She said there was a leather jacket on the arm of her chair. I then smelled manure. She told me she lived close to a pig farm, and the smell of manure is strong outside her home. Then I asked her if she had her legs crossed and if she was wearing white tennis shows. She was.

I never imagined that doing a psychic reading over the phone like this was possible for me. I was truly feeling like I had a psychic gift. I began to psychically read everyone I talked to. I felt this new interest was getting me headed in a more positive direction.

Chapter 24:
Reading People: A Blossoming Gift

I began to experiment regularly with my emerging psychic gift. For instance, one night, while my neighbor and I were out eating, I decided to talk to a group of diners at the next table over.

"Would you all like to play a game where I will psychically read something about you?" I asked them.

They were fair game, and I was excited because I was at the peak of my insight. So I closed my eyes and hit them with the first thing I saw: "Someone had a hard time picking out earrings earlier in today," I said.

One of the girls raised her hand.

"Someone is arguing with her mother. You better make up soon!"

Another girl said she was the one who had argued with her mother.

Next, I began to see a single rose, and the woman across from me pulled down the back of her shirt, revealing one red rose. That night, I read 15 things about the group, and 14 were correct.

We all decided to go over to the bar next door. Upon entering the establishment, I was instantly drawn to a table with six ladies. I knew I had to go and read them. So, I just asked if they would like to participate in a reading, and they thought it would be cool.

The first thing I saw was that someone was pregnant. The woman to my left said she had just found out she was expecting. I kept hearing the word "sisters," and I asked if that meant anything to the group. They responded that four of them were sisters. I also kept seeing skulls, and they told me they worked at a retirement home and they see people die often. I wasn't sure if that qualified as a hit, but they felt that it did.

I told them that I worked with a paranormal group in town, and they were excited because the founder of the group was a nurse at the retirement home. They knew him! I thought that it was an odd coincidence.

I ended my night being 95% connected with the women. Based on the night's experiences, I was high with wonder, and it was going to be hard to come down. I felt like I was going to burst. I wanted to tell people about what was happening. This went beyond recording audio of the dead, because it could be confirmed by real people.

The bar next to the restaurant.

That weekend we went up north to my mother-in-law's house, and that night I tried to read Mom and Dad. Everything I said connected with Dad, but I felt Mom was blocking me. Yes, I believe that individuals can intentionally block psychics from gaining information about them.

Dad knew I was on the right track. I told them that I kept seeing the springs that go on chicken coop doors. They revealed that they had just bought and installed the springs earlier that day. I had to be psychically connected or I couldn't be seeing these things, right?

The next day we were off to the museum. Before we left, I wrote down 15 things that I "saw" — things I knew we would encounter that day. I wrote my list and waited for them to come true. The first thing on my list was that I would see a brown purse with long straps. As soon as we got to the museum, a woman got out of her car with her new brown purse with long straps.

The next thing on my list was that I saw a person dropping change. As soon as we walked into the museum, someone dropped change by the gift store. I also had written that I would see a flag not flying but just lying flat against the pole. When we went to the car, we saw many flags blowing in the wind, except for one flag that hung tight against the pole.

There were a few more things that happened exactly as I had predicted and written down earlier that day. The last thing I saw was a belt with holes throughout, which was distinct-looking from most belts. Later that day, we pulled up to McDonald's and the girl that was giving us our food was wearing the exact belt I had described on my list.

Even though I hit on many things on the list I had made, no one seemed to care. And I admit that it did bother me a lot. It is a shame that a person can see the future, write it down beforehand, and watch it unfold as described only to be ignored. I didn't want to give up. I wanted to show my friends and family that these things were real. Psychic phenomena are real.

So, I decided to write a list on my way back home. I showed it to my sister-in-law before we began our journey home from the museum. I knew I would almost hit a bald eagle, and as I turned the corner there was an eagle eating a dead animal. I came within about two feet from hitting the eagle. Thirteen out of 14 things happened that I predicted. My sister-in-law was able to validate the results. But with all this proof, my wife still would not believe I had a psychic gift. I was starting to give up on sharing things with her.

Chapter 25:
Reading My Neighbor and Family

One night while I was at my neighbor's home, I shared with them the psychic phenomena that I was experiencing. My neighbor's wife wanted me to do a reading for her, so I told her to give me paper and pen and I would write what I saw.

I wrote about a bear rug, house with green shutters, a machete coming down, an "s" shape swirling in the air, and a few other details. Later that week, her grandpa passed on and she went up north to the funeral. The first thing she saw was the house with the green shutters. Also, at the funeral an argument broke out about her grandpa's bear rug. They were arguing about the bear rug on his casket. And at the hospital where her grandpa had died, they had just changed their logo to a floating, swirling "s."

Later that week, her brother-in-law called to say he was rescuing someone from a burning car and almost had to use his machete to cut off the trapped person's leg. Fortunately, it did not come to that. When my neighbor's returned that week from the funeral, they were blown away by how accurate my reading had been.

The simplest way I can describe my gift is like this: I see images in my mind or hear voices guiding me. I couldn't believe how accurate they always turned out to be. But I usually don't know what they mean until the person I am reading tells me.

The next weekend I called my sister. While talking, I began to tell her things that I was psychically seeing inside her home. She was shocked, as I had never visited her house before and had no way of knowing about the things I was describing.

What I found really cool was that I actually picked up her thoughts about dinner, what she had for breakfast, and what she was going to do the next day. Calling my family definitely was good for me, because after hearing my wife's response to what was happening to me really damaged my self-confidence. She was very negative about what I was doing. I never did understand her point of view, because I felt what was happening was very important and meant to happen just as it did.

My sister's home.

I decided that I wanted to use my gifts to help people. I even thought I might be able to help solve murder cases or other crimes. So, if I saw or read a news story about a crime, I would drive by those places to see what I could pick up psychically. Unfortunately, this method did not work like I thought it would. It seemed that my gift was restricted to having the person physically with me or on the phone in order to get their energy.

116

I had hoped that I would be able to touch an object or go to a site, feel the presence of the spirit, and talk to them to get answers about what happened. I had envisioned that when I gave these details to police, they would be astounded at how I could know details that I should not know. But, this scenario didn't become a reality for me, no matter how much I wanted to help.

This setback did not discourage me though. I kept doing what I had been doing, psychically tuning into what the next customer's house or conversation would be like. The next couple of days, I took my wife with me to my worksites. One day, we decided to stop by a yard sale.

"We are going to see a rocking horse," I told her on the way to the yard sale.

She laughed and said, "We will see."

When we got to the yard sale, my wife spotted the rocking horse. It was a toy rocking horse about six inches tall. But, my wife did not think that a toy rocking horse was a match for my vision. But why wouldn't it be a match? What I see in my mind's eye is a picture of an object. I don't usually see the exact size of the object. And sometimes what I see can have different meanings.

My wife still wanted to play "the game," so she decided she'd take her shot at a prediction. She said that before we arrived at my next job location, we would see a yellow cab. And right before we turned down the street to the client's house, we spotted a yellow cab at an auto shop.

She took satisfaction in showing me that these types of things were only based on luck and not on any type of psychic gift. Of course, I knew differently.

When we made it back home that day, I was feeling terrible, because I had been sensing a terrible event. I knew someone was going to have a horrible death the next day. When I told my wife about it, she told me to go to bed.

The next morning, a few miles away from our home, a man lost control of his vehicle, slid under a semi, and his upper half was cut off. Could I have saved his life? Probably not. I did not know his name or address. Or was there something earlier that day I should have paid attention to that could have saved him? I guess I will never know for sure. But, I did realize something about what was happening to me. I could feel really bad things psychically.

The following week I was recording in my van. I heard the van door open, and the light came on. I thought it was strange. However, I found out later that night after my recording, a young girl had been trying to shut her van door while on the road, fell out of the van, and lost her life. The accident occurred a few miles from where I lived. I wondered if I knew who was in trouble and when a tragedy was going to occur, could I help and actually make a difference?

I started sharing my experiences with my children, more and more each day. What I did not realize was how much my son was really taking it to heart. When I shared things with him about the paranormal, it stuck in his mind and never left him. He was like a sponge, soaking up everything. He is a very smart child, but he would get scared easily.

I wanted to alleviate his fears and show him that spirits are a part of our lives. I started having him take the recorder and walk through the house, not talking but just walking. When he got done, I would listen to the audio for spirit voices. And sure enough they were talking to him and even saying his name.

I wanted to prove to my wife that spirits do talk to people, even children, so I conducted another experiment. I began leaving the recorder in a room with my children. I would then retrieve the audio and listen. Many times I could hear voices on the recording that were not my children.

The voice of an old woman said, "Good little, tall girl."

I figured it was the proof I needed to convince my wife. I was wrong again. She refused to deal with the recording. I guess I was never going to get her to believe in the paranormal or my psychic gifts. I continued to record my kids and captured very interesting voices. The voices seemed to be random, and I wasn't sure if the spirits were directly connecting or if they were imprints in the atmosphere.

Chapter 26:
The Spiritual Center

I really needed to talk to someone about the psychic phenomena I was experiencing, so I called a spiritual center for help. John Davis was on the other line. He set up a meeting with me the following week after work.

When I arrived at the center, there was one vehicle in the parking lot. I went inside and saw a receptionist. I told her I had a meeting with their spiritual leader, and she asked me to wait for a minute. While waiting, I looked around at some brochures and began to read about the center. It was interesting because they based their beliefs on gifted individuals who could prove their talents. It dated back to the Gnostic and Coptic Christian Traditions of Egypt. One example is of an individual named Hamid Bey, who could do amazing things, including being buried underground for hours at a time, levitating his body, seeing the future and the past, and healing people.

The spiritual center where I met John.

I was very interested in this type of religion, because I built my faith on the same thing. I had captured a piece of audio that I thought needed to be brought to the spiritual leader's attention. It said, "Saint Peter, piece of me." It is a very religious quote, and I connected it to when Jesus sat at the Last Supper, blessed the bread, broke it, and told the Apostles to eat, saying, "This is my body."

When I entered John's office, I felt very comfortable. I told him about my life and the journey I was on. He told me about his own journey and where he was heading. He also gave me a numerology reading based on my name, birthday, and a few other factors. This type of reading is supposed to give you unique insight into your past, present, and future.

John told me I had lived three lives before, as a nun, a criminal, and a very shy person. What he was telling me was actually making sense to me. He told me I was more talented than many others that he knew, and I had an opportunity to do something with this talent to help people.

"Make a wish and write down 10 things you want to happen in your future. It will all come true," he said.

I wanted to believe him, but wasn't sure about what he said. I remained open-minded.

About six months went by, and my gift was getting stronger. I decided to meet with John at his office again to give him an update on my journey and some visions I had about him. I told of seeing sand; a convoy of trucks; big castles; a white bird flying high in the sky, looking down; and a holy man sitting high up on a cliff by himself.

John told me I was brought to him to share my visions of his upcoming trip to Egypt. This proved to me that it didn't matter if I could not understand my visions. The person I was reading would know what they meant.

John showed me a brochure that documented some of the talented people who he worked with, and he suggested I do the same. He said that these individuals charged so much per half hour for a reading and that I should create a profile about what I do and my abilities. He believed my business would grow fast, and I would make an extra income psychically reading people.

I liked the thought of helping people while also making a living at it. I could also hone my abilities at the same time. But, in the end, I decided to continue reading for free, as it felt like the right thing to do for me personally.

Chapter 27:
Making Mistakes

During my paranormal journey, I made many mistakes — as I revealed in the introduction to this book. I am about to tell you about another huge mistake I made: I used my gift at work on a job very close to my home. I went there to do a measure, and it never crossed my mind that I would get in trouble talking about the paranormal. The lady of the house mentioned that a contractor left the job to help find his missing niece. This seemed like an opening to tell her a little about myself, so I told her that I was almost on *The Montel Williams Show* to see psychic Sylvia Browne. I revealed to her that I can feel and hear things and often can record EVPs of spirits on my audio recorder.

"You can try my house if you want," she said.

I didn't see any harm in it since she offered, so I started walking through her home. I immediately felt my heart racing, like I was having a heart attack. I felt like I drank 10 cups of coffee. That is when she said her father had passed away, and he did often drink 10 cups of coffee in a day.

I walked through every room of the house, looking at pictures and trying to pick up the vibes. I listened to a few voices, but then it was time for me to head to my next job. The client must have told her husband about what happened, because he called my company and complained. And then he made another call. To the police.

My wife called me and said the police had shown up at our house. The woman's husband claimed that I scared her by talking about the spirits. I apologized and ensured the police that the woman did not appear frightened at the time or I would not have talked about the subject. I certainly did not mean to scare her and was sorry it had happened.

My paranormal obsession was causing serious problems for my family. I was telling my wife lie after lie to ensure her I was not using recorders or sharing my psychic gift with others. She was really scared, because this was hurting our business. And if I could not control myself, it would cost us greatly. My wife took my recorders away from me and hid them behind the books in the book case. I was not happy about it. I managed for a few days, but then I started missing my addiction again.

My wife hid my audio recorders behind
the books in our bookcase.

My wife couldn't keep the recorders hidden from me. It seemed like wherever she hid them, I was meant to find them. It didn't take me very long to find the recorders, so I was back at it again without her even knowing.

Unfortunately, it didn't take me long to forget the lesson I learned after talking to a client about my psychic journey. I thought I would read the next home I was working at. So I did, and I got six things right on the dot. But I made a huge mistake by showing my list of predictions to the customer. She went along and sounded excited about the psychic matches, but the next day she called my employer and complained. And, of course, I got another call from the big wigs at my job. They gave me a final warning not to talk about religion, or much of anything at all, or it would be my last job. I promised myself and my family I would never bring up the paranormal to clients again, and I stuck to my promise. Lesson learned ... finally.

From that point on, each time I thought a client would like to hear what I had to say about the paranormal, I remembered that not everyone believed in those types of things, or if they did believe, they associated it with evil or something bad. I also reminded myself of the times I was stabbed in the back after sharing information about my gifts with clients who seemed interested. In a strange twist, years later, clients started bringing up the paranormal to me.

I started watching TV shows and would often predict how a show would end. I would watch detective shows or psychic shows and put my two cents in before they would talk about the killer or the crime. I would even record the show, and then, while watching it back, I could hear spirits responding back to certain questions that I would ask.

At this point, I felt that my EVP recordings had run their course, but I was very in tune with my psychic abilities. I did still talk to friends and family about my readings. And I often offered to do a reading for them for free. Most of the time I was right on target, but other times I could not understand what I was seeing.

This gift takes time to understand. For instance, I told one woman I saw a small Poodle and she responded that she didn't have a Poodle. She had a Terrier that she was fond of. It seems that when I get these pictures, they are only part of the puzzle. I realized I needed more practice reading people. In essence, I needed training. It's like training to be a mechanic; you have to be tested and tested until you get the repair or procedure correct. I believe it is the same with spirits. You have to put the time in, practice, and even make mistakes along the way.

Connecting with spirits is like a relationship. The more time you spend with them, the better the results you get. I believe that everyone has a gift; they just have to put time into it for good results.

I made other mistakes and learned many lessons on my paranormal journey, including just how dangerous some locations can be. Sometimes it took a while for things to sink in, and other times I learned quickly.

The dangers of paranormal investigation are very real.

Chapter 28:
Seeing the Past by Touching Objects

An acquaintance of mine, who we'll call James, called and asked me to investigate his friend's home. Of course, I agreed, and we met up later that night. I gave him a recorder, and he went inside to record. I stayed outside so that I could also record. When he came back, we listened to the audio and heard a man screaming, saying that he was falling off the roof. I later found out that an apartment complex once existed in the location and a man did fall to his death from the building.

We also heard strange voices talking about the Devil and bad spirits. My acquaintance was extremely upset about what was on the recording. He was a big man and did not scare easily, but by the end of the night, he was frightened. I gave him one of the audio recorders to take home with him. He was going to try to connect with spirits at his home. James had the recorder for about a week and then brought it back to me so I could upload his audio onto my computer.

The apartment complex where a man fell to his death.

As I began to listen, I heard voices describing James' grandpa getting ill. *Oh no, not again,* I thought. Unfortunately, James' grandpa died about a week later.

James had a slight heart attack following our investigation and his attempts to record spirits. He was so distressed about what he recorded that he himself became ill. He stopped recording audio for good. I was upset that I had gotten him into this. But I never thought something like this would happen. Thankfully, James did not hold me responsible for any of the recent events. In fact, he heard me on a radio program, called in, and said some really kind things about me.

Our paths would cross again soon. A month later I went to pick up a pizza, and James was there. He had purchased some items at an antique store and wanted to know if they were real. So he asked me to take the objects home with me, do some audio recordings, and then let him know what I heard and felt.

Once I retrieved the items — a military war helmet from the 1940s and a military water container — from James and made it home, I began to record. As I did, I saw in my mind's eye that it was wartime. I saw a Nazi hat and a container. As I focused on the helmet, I saw an automatic rifle going off. I then changed my focus to the container. I saw some names and a man saying he was wounded. I decided to sleep with the objects to determine if I could see anything more. I held the container in my arms and wore the helmet as I slept.

I woke up the next morning with my T-shirt inside out and on backwards. I have no clue how or why this happened. But I would have had to take off the helmet and my shirt, turn the shirt inside out, put it on backwards, and put the helmet back on. That seemed unlikely. I recorded with the items for a few more nights, but nothing else happened. So I returned the goods to James and told him about my visions. I told him that I believed that every object has some kind of energy with it or around it, capturing its past.

One night soon after, I woke up to a very loud bang. It was a power line outside, and the surge went through our house and blew the microwave, automatic garage door opener, and computer. We took the computer for repairs, and they said everything on the computer was lost, including my audio. I was devastated to lose many of the EVPs and spirit voices that I had saved over the years.

Chapter 29:
Putting My Psychic Abilities to the Test

At about this time, paranormal shows started getting even more popular. I decided to call another show and tell them about my story and ability to capture spirit voices. I also asked if I could go on an investigation with them. They turned me down on both counts. They told me that just based on the fact that I could record spirits, they couldn't feature me on their show. They said that if I or my children were being haunted, they would come running. What I had to offer would not bring them ratings, and it seemed like that was all they focused on.

I decided to contact Puddin from the local radio station again to discuss my psychic abilities. Once I did, he and his co-host agreed to test me in their own way the next Friday. The night before the test, I wrote down my predictions. I would see a dog at the studio, see someone with a keychain around their belt loop, and hear someone talk about roof work, among other things.

When I got to the station on Friday, I made my way up to the 10th floor. As I came upon the receptionist, we began chatting. I connected with her psychically and instantly asked her if she had seen a rusty, old barrel. She had. Her dad had been burning wood in it. Matter of fact, she was talking about that same barrel earlier in the day. And as I was waiting for Puddin, the elevator door opened and out came a big dog.

Once I met with Puddin and his co-host, they read the list I had made the night before and had sent them prior to arriving at the station. They confirmed the information on the list that I had received psychically.

The building the radio station was located in.

Next up, another test. They held up five envelopes, each one holding a word or phrase. I had to guess what each word was, and if I got it wrong, I would be tasered or cattle prodded. Yes, I was that confident in my abilities that I agreed to be tasered if I was wrong!

I made my first guess, and it had something to do with leather. The second envelop had something to do with the color red. The third contained a word that had something to do with money. I can't remember what I guessed for envelops four and five, probably because I got them wrong.

The first word was "bondage," and they gave me that one because I had guessed the word leather, a common material for bondage products. The second phrase was "hot water bottle." They discussed my answer and decided to give it to me since many older hot water bottles were red. The third phrase was child molester. I missed that one, as well as the next two. I was not happy that I only picked up on two out of five envelops.

So, I was tasered. The first time, it barely worked. The next couple of times, it wasn't that bad. The last time, I was cattle prodded and, wow, did I feel that one! It went through my entire body and into my neck. To make the day even more painful, I had parked in the wrong space and been ticketed while I was on the show.

Some people said the radio show did me wrong. But I had agreed to it, so I took full responsibility. My wife and friends were quite mad because the DJs were basically laughing at me. But, if I am willing to do this, there will always be skeptics that will oppose it and disagree. Sometimes I am right. Sometimes I'm not. It seemed that every time I wanted someone to test my gifts, I was much less accurate. Maybe I wasn't supposed to prove my abilities to anyone. Maybe I was just supposed to help people with them.

I was at work when I got a call from one of my detective friends. He said a local magazine was looking for someone to talk to about the paranormal. So I called and talked to the reporter and set up an interview with her. Because I was very busy with my job that day, the reporter agreed to meet me at a nearby restaurant. We had coffee and then I began telling her my story. She seemed interested in and even impressed with what I was saying. She said she would call me in a week, and if I received any visions to pass them on to her.

For some reason, I knew this would not pan out. I read her and sent her my findings the next week. But I never heard from her again. Did she lose interest? Did I hit the nail on the head and upset her with my visions? Or did I get everything entirely wrong? I would never know.

I started watching more ghost shows. One show featured animals sensing ghosts at an old tavern where a mob criminal had been murdered. During the episode, a paranormal team came in to help. But I was unhappy with their results. The next day I called the tavern and offered my help, but in a different way. I said if they would talk on the speakerphone, I would record them and send them back proof of paranormal activity within the hour. They turned me down.

I started contacting ghost hunters around the United States, offering to provide them proof that their audio recordings captured more than what they had heard themselves. Sometimes groups would email me back, but then the contact would die out.

During this time, I took my kids sledding with my neighbor. As we were heading home, it was dark out. I told them that as soon as we passed my street, they should look down the road at the lights. They would see one go off. As soon as we passed, a light went off. Then I told my neighbor to watch a specific light that was off. I told him I would count to seven and command the light to turn on. When what I said unfolded exactly as I had said it would, he was shocked.

While I had been learning not to share my gifts with everyone, my neighbor was a trusted friend. I had learned that telling the wrong person about my gifts could lead to major problems. And while a lot of people were getting more interested in the paranormal, I also knew that many would never truly be connected or accept the possibilities of our world.

I believe you must be completely open to all possibilities and/or have a real gift to be a success at paranormal investigation. Spirits like to react to someone who really wants to hear them, and not just for TV show ratings.

As the years passed by, I noticed more and more people becoming engrossed in and even obsessed with the paranormal. I was finding more Websites online about the paranormal and spirit contact. I was also finding more information about police working with psychics to solve murders or search for missing people.

The increased interest in the paranormal excited me. I was thinking about reaching out again, because now a lot more people were open to the possibilities of paranormal and psychic activity. I found a new paranormal Website, and I began loading my evidence to the site. I put about a dozen videos on it and started getting responses immediately.

I also put up a discussion thread on the site's forum. I offered to read the members of the site — past, present, and future. I started getting responses and began reading people. I did get some hits on the first few people I read. But, I found that the more people I read, the more hits I was getting. I was appreciative that I was able to practice my gift while trying to provide insights to others. As I said before, it was like training and honing my talents. The more I trained, the more everything fell into place.

So I started doing readings on the Internet to anyone who wanted one. The responses that I got were amazing. People really wanted a free reading, and they were piling up.

Chapter 30:
Murder Victim Research

One morning, I went into a home to do a job close to my town, and as soon as I stepped inside the house, something began bothering me. As I began to do my job, the feeling of someone watching me was strong. It was so strong that I mentioned my unease to the owner of the home. I told her that her house freaked me out. I knew I was dangerously close to breaking my rule of not talking about the paranormal with clients, but I felt compelled to say something.

She laughed and said she was a psychic and had worked with the police on solving crimes. She told me it was a ghost that was visiting her that I was feeling. So we talked for a while about her gifts, and I did reveal that I had some experience in the field. As I was leaving, she told me about an unsolved case involving a missing girl. The girl came to her and told her where she could be found and who had killed her. I was very interested in what she had to say, and I gave her my number. I knew this client would not be calling my employer to complain about me.

As she shook my hand, she told me that one day I would not need the recorder to communicate with spirits and that my psychic abilities would grow to be very strong. Later, she called and asked me about two names that she saw when she shook my hand. The names were the middle names of my son and wife.

I felt in my heart she was the real deal. There was no way she could have known what she told me. This was the start of a new friendship. She asked me to try and see if I could hear the missing girl's voice in the area where she went missing. I was excited to try and help. I believed this was the right path for me.

The next chance I had, I went to the school where the girl went missing. It was daytime and school was in session. There was a road that went between the high school and the middle school. I drove around, down each nearby street, recording audio while doing so. As soon as I was done, I listened to the audio.

I heard a girl say, "It's me, Dawn."

I then heard a lot of cursing, and I got references to the missing girl's dad and her friends' names. At the time, I didn't know I had caught the names of her friends. I found that out later. I got home that night and loaded the audio onto my computer. Then I sent the audio to my new psychic friend. She listened to the audio and was blown away. While she already knew a lot about the missing girl, she had not known much about her friends.

The school the missing girl attended.

After hearing what I had captured, she gave me a phone number to one of the missing girl's childhood friends and to a lady who used to babysit her. I called the former babysitter of the missing girl and told her what I did. I also told her about the information I had captured during my investigation. She agreed to meet with me at her house. It was the following Wednesday around one o'clock when I met with her and the childhood friend of the missing girl.

Over the phone I told the former babysitter, "When I get there, please don't speak right away. Spirits have a message as soon as I come in. Sometimes they're angry and say they don't want me around, and sometimes they will invite me in."

On the day of the meeting, I entered the location with my recorder on. As soon as I walked in, I began to walk around asking for the missing girl's spirit to come and communicate with me. It only took five minutes. After reviewing the audio, as I stepped into the dining room, a voice came on and said something. I heard it right away. The former babysitter heard it right away too. She actually fell back on her couch once she heard the voice.

The young girl's voice said, "Come find me," almost like the spirit was playing a game of hide and seek.

After that day, I asked if I could return and record more audio. They allowed me to return and investigate again. At one point during my return investigation, I sat down with the babysitter, and she told me the story of what had happened. It seems that one winter day during a wrestling match at the school, the young girl asked her mother to use the restroom. She left, and no one saw her again. She was 13 years old.

I was recording during our entire discussion. Afterwards, they wanted to take me to the school, to one of her friend's house, and to the victim's house. I thought this might be a good way to solve a mystery that was more than 27 years old. When I got done with all of the recordings at the various locations, I went home and loaded all the recordings onto my computer. I was very interested in listening and hoping I could get the clue to bust the case wide open.

That night was a long one. I listened to the audio after my family went to bed. I listened until about four in the morning. Having to get up at 6 a.m. for work, my wife was getting concerned about my continual lack of sleep.

When I contacted the babysitter and the victim's best friend again with my results, we set up another meeting and went over all of the captured audio. I did capture many spirit voices on the recordings, but we found no real clues to help solve the case. I still didn't give up. I tried many times to reach the young girl, hoping that she would give me what I needed to find her. But it was a long road.

I did capture some names and direct information about the girl. I asked my psychic friend if I should go to the police with the details I had captured on my audio recording, and she said it wouldn't hurt. So I planned that Friday to get up enough nerve to talk to the police.

When I arrived at the sheriff's station, the officers assigned to the case weren't there. So, I gave the desk clerk a compact disc and a handwritten list of the audio on the disc that related to the missing girl's case. The clerk said she would give the information to the detectives that were on the case.

I had to wait weeks before I could return to the sheriff's station to try to talk to the detectives. When I finally did, they said they couldn't hear anything on the audio. I told them that they would be able to hear the voices if they were in a quiet room with headphones. They asked me if I had some kind of medical paper showing that I could hear ghost voices. I told that I did not, but when I was younger, I had Bell's palsy. The left side of my face went numb, and my hearing was heightened immensely. I could hear a pin drop in another room.

They told me they would try to listen to the audio again. They also said I could go to the school anytime to try and reach the missing girl and that the police would not bother me if I told them the detectives allowed me to do it. I took their advice and kept doing what I was doing, still hoping for that clue that would help solve the crime. Unfortunately, the case remains unsolved as of this writing.

Chapter 31:
Continuing My Search for the Missing

I ultimately conducted more psychic investigations on my own. And years after the missing girl's case, I began researching another missing person's case. I was at a job site on the east side of my town, and while talking to the homeowner she brought up a missing person's case. She told me that he was an older man who had enough money to live on. It seemed odd to me that someone like that would just run off. *Not likely*, I thought.

The case kept nagging at me, so I decided to look up the missing man's brother in the phonebook. I called him and left a message, telling him about how I do audio recordings and that sometimes I can connect with spirits. I told him I might be able to help. I did not think he would call me back, but he did.

When he called, I told him what I did, and he said he would like to meet me at his missing brother's house. I was excited, but at the same time scared. It is always a touchy subject to talk to people about a loved one who has passed on, and especially those who passed on in tragic circumstances. Was I really doing the right thing? What if I couldn't help? Did I just get this man's hopes up?

We agreed to meet that Sunday, and I was very nervous. I was not just recording random voices; I was dealing with the spirits of loved ones who had gone missing. As I pulled up the dirt and gravel road that Sunday, I started recording. The house was up on a hill on the left, and there were two vehicles there. I got out and two of the missing man's brothers were there, along with a friend who was a detective. The detective's niece was the best friend of the missing girl who I had researched years ago. A strange coincidence.

We all walked into the mobile home, hoping I could connect. We started by the back bedroom where the missing man slept and then continued with the rest of the home, finishing in the kitchen. I went outside and around the trailer and recorded. When I got to the front, I felt as if someone was choking me. It was so real that it almost took my breath away.

When I went back to the car, I told everyone what had happened. It was then that they told me another psychic who investigated the case also picked up on the missing man being choked. We ended up taking a ride down the road to the post where they believed he had been taken. I recorded in the hope of capturing spirit voices.

The road I took to the missing man's trailer to meet his brother.

We got down to the end of the road, and we came across a hunter. The men talked to him about their missing brother, but he didn't know anything about it. Then we walked down another path and talked more about other people who were interested in the case. When we finished up that day, it was time to analyze the recordings I had collected.

That night I stayed up late hoping to connect with the missing man. I immediately knew he had passed away. I captured audio of a man stuttering and talking about being hit. He was saying things that I didn't understand at the time. When we all met up again, I gave the missing man's brother a CD of the audio and a list of everything I psychically connected to regarding his brother. Later that day, he called me to confirm that the information I provided him matched things about his brother that I could not have known about.

This investigation started me in new direction. I began to help families search for their missing relatives. I continued to put in a lot of time into the case of the missing man, hoping to get results. Little did I know how much I eventually did get right.

I continued to meet up with the two brothers to record and try to find their missing brother. I would usually call my wife and tell her I was running late, more lies. During one investigation, we walked back into the woods and recorded audio. We all spread out at the location, asking questions and hoping to capture answers. We all went in different directions and then met in the middle. We then met back at the trailer, where I left one recorder in the house.

This time the audio revealed more signs of a struggle and where he was taken from. We captured one audio that said he was located northeast. There were a lot of voices that didn't make sense on the audio, and we didn't know what to think because he was still missing.

147

Later that week, the brothers bought me a new audio recorder. I didn't tell my wife. So I had two recorders that she didn't know about. Even though I was lying to my wife, I still felt my research was the right thing to do. After all, I was trying to help people.

I again met with the brothers and utilized my spirit board and audio recorder. Using the spirit board was new to me. Did it really work, or was it really just a game? After we conducted our session, I went back home to listen to my audio.

At this point, my wife didn't want me investigating anymore, so I couldn't do the evidence review at my house, only in secret. Sometimes, I would take the kids to the park and review it while they were playing. A lot of times while on the road I would to listen to my recorder. There were times I would do it at home while everyone else was in bed.

I even began telling my wife that I was going to the bar, but in reality I was going over to the property near where we thought the missing man's body was taken.

I would go down by the river and ask the spirits questions. I asked if they could help me find this missing person. I would get replies such as, "He was hit on the head by a big man" and "We dragged him." I took it to mean there were two individuals involved in the crime. I could hear the victim say, "Please don't hurt me."

All these things had an effect on my life. By the river where I had been many times, I still remember that old black bridge I could see from a distance. I knew it meant something. This case was taking over my every waking moment. I would talk to the victim's brother almost daily, trying to figure who did it and where the body was.

On one of my audio recordings, I heard a spirit say the name of the perpetrator. And I psychically felt they poured something on the victim's body that would completely disintegrate it.

During this time, I would occasionally meet up with other psychically gifted people. Before each meeting, I would get visions of what I would see at the meetings or what would be said. I would see the types of clothing people would wear or objects that would be at the meeting.

During our gatherings, there was a very talented person who had visions about a previous case I had worked on. She would light candles and talk to the spirits, and they would respond by moving the flame. During one meeting, as the night went on, we listened to this woman describing her visions of each missing person's case. A lot of the details she came up with matched my findings exactly. Most of my findings were from audio, and her findings were from visions. Of course, I shared my recordings with the group. We all left our group sessions feeling like we were accomplishing something.

I continued to investigate the sites involved in the missing man's case. I kept looking for clues. But as time went on, it seemed like the spirits were giving me false information. For instance, I would ask, "Who killed you?" and I would hear different names upon playback of the audio.

I met up with the brothers of the missing man again, and I gave them another CD of the audio I captured and a written transcript of what was said on the CD.

This case did have a resolution. The authorities ended up convicting two men for the missing man's murder. Coincidentally, I had previously worked inside one of the murderer's houses for my company. I wondered why I hadn't picked up psychic impressions about the man during my work on his property. But, I did hope that I had helped in some small way with this case.

Chapter 32:
A Desire to Help

One evening I was watching the news and heard of another murder in the area, so I thought I would try to help. I went across town and started recording at the location where she lived and where, ultimately, she died. I captured audio indicating how she died, who did it, and how it happened.

The victim lived on the northeast side. One night she went for a walk and went missing, until they found her body naked in the park. They figured the crime had happened close to her home and that someone had kidnapped, raped, and killed her. I called her brother and offered my services, but he never called me back.

I wanted to help so badly that I was constantly reaching out to people. Unfortunately, some thought I was "crazy," which is unfortunate. But I never pushed anyone into talking with me. When I would not get a response, I stopped calling.

But, at the same time, I still kept recording on my own to see if I could uncover anything that might help the case. It was strange, but I always felt a connection to these missing people, and I always will. When the voices came through, they really touched my heart. I really felt they were reaching out to me.

Some of the audio I captured included, "A buddy came over and hit me on the head," "He was religious," and "He drove a truck." I sent these recordings to the police department but never heard back. I figured they probably were approached like this all the time — people claiming they had a gift, but instead it turned out to be just a wild goose chase.

The park where the body of a missing woman was found.

I never knew what the woman looked like until she was on the news. She was very pretty. I wondered how anyone could harm one of God's children.

After turning my evidence over to the police, I moved on to another case I heard about on the news. An older lady went missing from an arts and crafts store. After hearing about her last whereabouts on the news, I decided to try and make contact. I went everywhere the missing woman was sighted — her work, where they found her purse, and where they found her car.

Instantly, I heard, "He broke my hand." Then I heard her say her husband's name. I really didn't know if the messages were from the missing woman, but a few of the details I heard did match with her case. I would drive by the area weekly, hoping for that one piece of evidence that the police could use to help solve the case, but that never happened. I did fax all the information I obtained on the case to the police. I even called one day and told them, "You will find her on the thirteenth." And sure enough they did.

But nobody seemed to care much about my investigations. I was pretty much ignored, especially by the police. This did not bother me, because I still wanted to make any kind of effort to communicate and help loved ones if they wanted me to. I made up my mind to do this until the missing people were found, or their bodies were found.

So I continued to watch the news every day, hoping I could help in some way. Then I became aware of a murder that was about 100 miles away from where I lived. A little girl had been killed in a graveyard. A couple of weeks later, I had a job just a few miles away from the crime scene. I had a half hour before my next job, so I decided to run to the graveyard and take a look.

I started down the street where I believe she lived and headed for the cemetery. I did my usual routine of asking the victim to communicate. I asked questions about what happened to her, if she knew who was involved, and what the perpetrator looked like.

Later, I listened to the audio and was shocked to hear a young girl say, "Willie Manns kidnapped me." As I was heading back home, I called the local police department and let them hear what I had recorded. They wanted me to come down and let them hear it. So the following week I went down and played the recording for the chief of police. He could hear that there was something on the audio, but was it really her saying her killer's name?

He checked on the Internet for anyone with that name and nothing came up. He called in another investigator who listened as well, and she agreed with me on what it had said. I waited outside while they talked it over. They finally agreed to take me to a few

153

places where the crime had occurred. I was excited because I had never gone anywhere with the police before to investigate a case.

She took me to a bar downtown first and then to an electric plant. We walked all around as I asked for the little girl to speak with me. Then we went to the last place she was seen, and I felt a major headache coming on. The detective told me that is where the victim was last seen on her bike. Next, we went to the graveyard. I could tell that the detective wanted me to tell her where the body was found, but I could not. Then we went back to the station to assess the audio.

Where the missing girl's body was found.

But, the chief appeared and cut our time short. He said he could hear the amount of syllables, but he could not make out what it really said. So I said I would take my recorder home and leave one for the detective. When I left I was relieved. It had never occurred to me until then that the police might think I was involved with the crime!

When I got home that night, I made it a priority to transcribe the audio recordings. I did so and sent them to the chief. But something odd occurred that had never happened before. New voices appeared on the recordings that hadn't been there the first time I listened. One was describing a brick house and another was saying, "Home on Depot Street." Other EVPs said, "Blood was in the hair" and "A lonely man kidnapped me."

I didn't know what to make of the audio recordings changing. How was that possible? I started to check some of my other audio recordings, and sure enough, some of those had changed as well. I couldn't figure out why this would happen.

I waited for a call back from the police, and sure enough it never came. About a week later I saw a story on the little girl's case on the news. The police were now asking all the men in town to give the department a sample of their DNA.

I continued to record in the areas where the little girl was murdered, but she started to fade away. It was almost like she got her message out and when no one would believe her, she faded.

It still hurt deeply when no one seemed to listen to what the spirits were saying. But, it was at this point in my journey that I decided I would always try and help the spirits. If no one else would listen to them, I would. Maybe, if I at least listened, the spirits would have some peace in the afterlife.

Chapter 33:
My Journey Continues

Today, I still investigate the paranormal and continue on my paranormal journey. While my obsession isn't as intense, it hasn't died out. The paranormal will always be a big part of my life, as I believe it is a part of everyone's life, whether they realize it or not.

And as time goes by, the paranormal field will grow and become more accepted. It has already come a long way from where it used to be. Not as many people are as quick to label psychics or paranormal investigators as "crazy." They are not as quick to roll their eyes.

I believe that, eventually, we all come together and have a big, old, happy reunion with all of our friends and loved ones. Maybe Heaven is just a wall that gets thinner every day, and maybe we get closer to being with our loved ones once and for all.

Thank you for sharing my paranormal journey with me.

My paranormal journey continues ...

Acknowledgements

I want to thank all of my friends and family who supported me on my paranormal journey. I also want to thank those who I met along the way. I want to mention a few individuals by name who helped me personally during my journey:

* My wife, Anne, stuck with me during my journey. She took care of her duties, as well as mine when I was not able to do them because of my obsession. Without her support during those early days, there might not have been a journey at all.

* Andrew Prater, my son, went on many ghost hunts with me. He helped me with many different experiments and not once did he complain about any of it.

* Todd Bates listened to me and helped me understand what was happening to me. He gave me great advice, which proved to be correct.

* Michael Stoll listened to me and helped with the first editing of my book.

* Alan Stoll helped me research many places. He gave me great advice on the way to do certain things that would help me in my journey.

* Kathy Conder helped me with my confidence. She took me to places, tested me, and invited me to her paranormal conferences where I learned so much.

* Leitreanna T. Brown was a great friend and listener when I needed someone. She also connected me to my publisher.

* Vic Weeks listened to me, believed in me, and always gave me positive feedback. He was always there when I needed someone to talk to. Never once did he say he did not have time for me. He took care of me like a son.

About the Author

Rick Waid is a seer, remote viewer, and past-life reader. He was born with gifts that he did not realize he had until his late-30s. While Rick's mother was also a reader, he did not become aware of his talents until he began researching the paranormal.

Rick began to connect with the other side through Electronic Voice Phenomena (also known as EVP), and he started having visions and hearing his spirit guide.

As his gift progressed, he learned how to remote view and was able to psychically see places he had never visited before. As Rick's gifts continued to evolve, he began to see past lives of individuals. He can also now connect with "the other side" and frequently receives messages from loved ones beyond the veil.

Rick wrote *My Paranormal Journey: One Man's Obsession* to share with others a compelling passion that ultimately revealed to him gifts he never knew he had.

"I hope it will help others realize there are reasons for exploring into new territories and breaking through current boundaries," Rick said.

CPSIA information can be obtained
at www.ICGtesting.com
Printed in the USA
LVHW080502150419
614187LV00031B/608/P

9 781508 706939